EDI DEVELOPMENT STUDIES

The Distribution of Income and Wealth in Korea

Danny M. Leipziger
David Dollar
Anthony F. Shorrocks
Su-Yong Song

The World Bank
Washington, D. C.

The Economic Development Institute (EDI) was established by the World Bank in 1955 to train officials concerned with development planning, policymaking, investment analysis, and project implementation in member developing countries. At present the substance of the EDI's work emphasizes macroeconomic and sectoral economic policy analysis. Through a variety of courses, seminars, and workshops, most of which are given overseas in cooperation with local institutions, the EDI seeks to sharpen analytical skills used in policy analysis and to broaden understanding of the experience of individual countries with economic development. Although the EDI's publications are designed to support its training activities, many are of interest to a much broader audience. EDI materials, including any findings, interpretations, and conclusions, are entirely those of the authors and should not be attributed in any manner to the World Bank, to its affiliated organizations, or to members of its Board of Executive Directors or the countries they represent.

Because of the informality of this series and to make the publication available with the least possible delay, the manuscript has not been edited as fully as would be the case with a more formal document, and the World Bank accepts no responsibility for errors.

The material in this publication is copyrighted. Requests for permission to reproduce portions of it should be sent to the Office of the Publisher at the address shown in the copyright notice above. The World Bank encourages dissemination of its work and will normally give permission promptly and, when the reproduction is for noncommercial purposes, without asking a fee. Permission to copy portions for classroom use is granted through the Copyright Clearance Center, 27 Congress Street, Salem, Massachusetts 01970, U.S.A.

The backlist of publications by the World Bank is shown in the annual *Index of Publications*, which is available from Distribution Unit, Office of the Publisher, The World Bank, 1818 H Street, N.W., Washington, D.C. 20433, U.S.A., or from Publications, Banque mondiale, 66, avenue d'Iéna, 75116 Paris, France.

Danny M. Leipziger is lead economist, David Dollar is senior country economist, and Su-Yong Song is an economist in the World Bank's East Asia and Pacific—Country Department I. Anthony F. Shorrocks is professor of economics at the University of Essex, United Kingdom.

Library of Congress Cataloging-in-Publication Data

The distribution of income and wealth in Korea / Danny M. Leipziger ... [et al.].
        p. cm.—(EDI development studies)
    Includes bibliographical references (p.   )
    ISBN 0-8213-2124-2
    1. Income distribution—Korea (South) 2. Wealth—Korea (South)
  3. Taxation—Korea (South) I. Leipziger, Danny M. II. Series.
HC470.I5L58 1992
339.35195—dc20   92-14468
                                                    CIP

EDI Catalog No. 405/061

CONTENTS

FOREWORD

The development experience of the Republic of Korea is perhaps the most studied case of the post-war era, and the World Bank has drawn heavily on that experience in advising other developing countries. The issue of income distribution has been a central theme in Korea's role as a development paradigm. As Korea approaches developed country status, however, it has begun to face new and unique development challenges. In order to continue to learn from the Korean case, the Bank's East Asia Department I initiated a study of the distribution of income and wealth, with the aim of learning further from one of its most successful members. This study, under the direction of Danny Leipziger, breaks new ground in fostering our understanding of these issues in rapidly growing economies.

Amnon Golan
Director
Economic Development Institute

ACKNOWLEDGMENTS

The authors, Danny M. Leipziger, David Dollar, and Su Yong Song of the World Bank and Anthony Shorrocks of the University of Essex, express their appreciation to Etisham Ahmad, Kwang Choi, Wontack Hong, Kyung-Hwan Kim, Soonwon Kwon, Emmanuel Jimenez, Tae Il Lee, Sang Woo Nam, and Jae-Young Son as well as to the attendees of the KDI seminar held in Seoul (May 1991) for valuable comments and to the officials of various government ministries and research institutes, especially the Economic Planning Board, Ministry of Finance, Korea Development Institute, Korea Research Institute for Human Settlements, Ministry of Construction, Office of National Tax Administration, and the Bank of Korea, as well as Citizens National Bank and Daewoo Securities, for their assistance. All views expressed are solely those of the authors and do not necessarily reflect the opinions of the World Bank or its affiliates. Thanks is due to Mercedes Pendleton for expertly typing the manuscript.

ABBREVIATIONS AND
CURRENCY EQUIVALENTS

BOK	Bank of Korea
CHIES	City Household Income and Expenditure Survey
CNB	Citizens National Bank
CPCLO	Commission on the Public Concept of Land Ownership
CPI	Consumer Price Index
EPB	Economic Planning Board
FHES	Farm Household Expenditure Survey
GDP	Gross Domestic Product
GNP	Gross National Product
HCI	Heavy and Chemical Industry
KDI	Korea Development Institute
KRIHS	Korea Research Institute for Human Settlements
OECD	Organisation of Economic Co-operation and Development
ONTA	Office of National Tax Administration
POSCO	Pohang Iron and Steel Company
UNDP	United Nations Development Programme
VAT	Value Added Tax

Currency Equivalents
(as of April 1992)

Currency Unit = Korean won (W)
US$1.00 = W775
W 1,000 = US$ 1.29

AN OVERVIEW

The growth performance of the Korean economy is perhaps unparalleled in the development history of the postwar period. The remarkable feature of Korea's growth record during the 1960s and 1970s was its distinct emphasis on equality in the sharing of income gains. Beginning with drastic land reform in the aftermath of the Japanese occupation, a pattern of urbanization and expansion of labor-intensive manufactures led to sharp increases in wage incomes, spread across a broad spectrum of society. The development literature is replete with studies of Korea's equitable growth record, and indeed its gains in welfare have been substantial by almost any measure.

The mid-1980s marked a turning point in Korea's history, when several major factors altered its traditional pattern of development. First, the process of democratization led to significant upheaval in labor markets, with widespread strikes, unionization activity, and greater public accountability of the distribution of gains. Related to this process—and the sharp reversal of Korea's external indebtedness, as epitomized by the appreciating won—was a new emphasis on consumption. This behavioral change revealed larger disparities in purchasing power than were previously realized. Nowhere was this lack of concordance between public expectations and actual purchasing power more apparent than in housing. This problem is starkly illustrated by the fact that wages have increased three-and-a half times compared with the average consumption basket since 1974 but have remained virtually unchanged in relation to housing costs.

The perception that the economic gains of Korea's rapid growth have not been fairly enough distributed is, it can be argued, causing difficulties in the labor market, where workers are not merely trying to capture productivity gains in their wage settlements, but are also trying to appropriate a portion of the gains they feel have eluded them in the past. The effect of wage settlements averaging 20 percent increases in both 1988 and 1989 led to sizeable difficulties in some manufacturing sectors and, when combined with exchange rate developments since the Plaza Accord, led to the disappearance of Korea's large current account surplus. The perception that income and wealth are becoming highly concentrated in Korea has also fueled public debates on tax policies, credit and refinancing for the agricultural sector, housing policies, and expenditure priorities. Government has indicated that dealing with this perception is one of its highest priorities because it is complicating the task of economic management.

The Distribution of Income

There are at least three reasons why one would not expect to be concerned about Korea's income distribution. First and foremost, the absolute gains in income have been extremely impressive. Per capita consumption growth increased by 5.6 percent annually in real terms between 1965 and 1985. Second, absolute poverty, which affected 40 percent of the population in 1965, was reduced to 10 percent in 1980 and its incidence has continued to fall. Third, by all official accounts, the actual distribution of income remained virtually unchanged over the 1965-1985 period, with some actual gains reported since 1980. Why then is the public perception different?

Evidence points to a number of culprits, among them the quality of the data and the sampling techniques that traditionally have been employed. Between 1963 and 1977, for example, annual income surveys excluded all households on public assistance as well as those with incomes above a certain level. Although surveys conducted since 1980 did not deliberately exclude any group, two sampling defects remain: (1) the urban survey does not include income data for the self-employed and employer households, relying instead on expenditure data to calculate income; and (2) the rural survey does not include rural, nonagricultural households. Together, it is estimated that 40 percent of Korean households are excluded from the City Household Income and Expenditure Survey (CHIES) and Farm Household Expenditure Survey (FHES). Therefore, the official Economic Planning Board (EPB) statistics, which show improvements in the Gini coefficient between 1980 and 1988 (greater equality), can be viewed with some skepticism.

The Korea Development Institute (KDI) attempted to improve the sampling approach with its own survey for 1988. In particular, it attempted to oversample the low-income groups to get a representative national sample. Its findings that the lowest 40 percent of the income distribution received 15 percent of income compared with the official estimate of 20 percent reveal a significant difference for the bottom income groups. The KDI findings for the top 20 percent of the distribution show that the top earners received 47 percent of income, compared with 42 percent in the government survey. If shifts in the middle four deciles are marginal, there appears to be a pattern of greater inequality present than is revealed in the official income estimates.

One question that remains unanswered is whether the distribution of income, perhaps more unequal than first thought, has deteriorated over time. To begin to analyze this issue, a comparison was performed between the income data by source reported in the KDI survey and that reported in the national income accounts, as normally reported by the Bank of Korea. The aggregate income differs by only 13 percent, but the amounts reported for interest and dividends (returns to capital) in the KDI income survey are only one-fourth the amount calculated in the national income accounts. Because the holdings of capital assets are predominantly a feature of upper-income households, the underreporting of three-quarters of income derived from capital assets indicates that even the KDI survey is not satisfactorily capturing the income picture of the wealthier households. The only way to get a better handle on this phenomenon is to investigate the distribution of wealth, a very data-intensive, technical exercise.

The Distribution of Wealth

Measuring the holdings of personal wealth is a very difficult task. It is made even more challenging in the Korean context by the lack of comprehensive data. The single exception is a 1988 survey conducted by the KDI, which at least provides a benchmark against which other more fragmentary data can be analyzed. Comparisons of the Gini coefficient of inequality for income of .40 based on the KDI income survey with values of .58 for gross personal wealth, .60 for real assets, and .77 for financial assets reveal that *wealth is much more highly concentrated than income*. This is a phenomenon that prevails in most societies. Nevertheless, it is noteworthy that based on this sample of over 4,000 households, 43 percent of wealth is in the hands of the top 10 percent of households, 31 percent in the hands of the top 5 percent, and 14 percent in the hands of the top 1 percent. The statistics were estimated using a Pareto distribution, the best practice approach to completing wealth distribution from sample surveys.[1]

Comparisons between countries are fraught with difficulties because of variations in sampling techniques and other country-specific data peculiarities. Nevertheless, it is worth noting that Korea's distribution of wealth (1988 KDI survey) most resembles France's distribution in 1975. Because the composite wealth distribution contains wide discrepancies in the holdings of financial and land assets, a decomposition approach is followed. The two official sources of financial holdings are regular surveys by the Bank of Korea (BOK) and the Citizen's National Bank (CNB). These data have been converted in distributions, and along with estimates by Kang (1990), form a fairly consistent picture of financial holdings using *reported* holdings of financial assets.

The largest discrepancy between reported holdings and actual holdings occurs in land and real estate. The skyrocketing prices for land in recent years prompted Government to form the Commission on the Public Concept of Land Ownership (CPCLO). According to CPCLO's data, based on surveys of over 1 million land parcels and a very conservative (low) estimate of land prices, the value of land in 1988 was 216.2 trillion won, or $300 billion. If, as is widely acknowledged, land prices are really two or three times higher, the total value of landholdings may be equal to multiples of gross national product (GNP). There can be no doubt that the most valuable tangible assets in Korea today are in the form of land, and that this has significant implications for housing, income distribution, and industrial location.

---

1. The Pareto distribution, which has been shown to provide the best fit for the top quartile of the wealth distribution, is a logarithmic transformation of the frequency and size of wealth holdings.

Using data collected by CPCLO, it can be seen that in Seoul proper only 28 percent of households own land. In other words, 72 percent own no land at all. Among landowners, 62 percent of households own 34 percent of the land in Seoul, and the top 10 percent own 66 percent of the land. This pattern is repeated in all the large cities in Korea. Looked at from the vantage point of the Gini coefficient, it measures 0.85 for landowners.[2]

The distribution of landownership in Korea is a sensitive issue because land values have been rising rapidly for more than a decade. Between 1974 and 1989, for example, land prices rose by a factor of 14, more than three times as fast as real GNP. As a result, huge capital gains (unrealized as well as actual) have accrued to those owning these assets, a group that is a small fraction of the population. *Capital gains from landownership in 1989, for example, exceeded GNP.* Under these circumstances, income distribution data that fail to capture accurately the gains from land and real estate holdings will yield a biased view of the equity situation in the country. For this reason, further analysis was undertaken to construct a balance sheet of personal wealth for Korea.

The problem with sample surveys of wealth holdings is that wealthier households are more likely to refuse to cooperate, as well as being more likely to undervalue what they do report. In much the same way that national income accounts are constructed, a balance sheet for wealth is constructed using estimated values of the components of wealth (most markedly affected by land valuation). Using the most likely (middle) estimate for land values, total personal wealth exceeds 700 trillion won, of which more than 60 percent is attributable to land, and household wealth is found to be high by international standards. In addition, both the BOK and KDI surveys are thought to severely underestimate holdings of financial assets, and the KDI survey, which covers real assets, is thought to underestimate land and real estate holdings by a quarter. To remedy the sample selection and undervaluation biases, adjustments were made to the KDI survey, making a variety of alternative assumptions about reporting behavior. An intermediate adjustment rule assumes that all households undervalue assets by 10 percent and that all remaining reporting

---

2. Gini coefficients range from zero (perfect equality) to 1.0 (perfect inequity).

discrepancies reflect holdings of the richest households. That this adjustment raises the wealth holdings of the top decile from 43 percent to 49 percent of personal wealth highlights the importance government should attach to improving reporting of wealth statistics.

Taxation of Income and Wealth

Korea's tax system is a generally efficient one, capable of raising revenue, and at least by design, providing some progressivity. The tax structure, it is fair to say, takes as its primary objective the raising of revenue rather than the redistribution of income. Nevertheless, by initial design, and with reforms such as those recommended by the Commission on Tax Reform 1985,[3] it has taken the objectives of horizontal and vertical equity as functional principles. It is therefore a valid concern of policymakers to investigate how well these objectives are being met.

Korea's overall tax burden, as measured by taxes collected as a fraction of GNP, is on par with other rapidly growing economies of Asia; the tax system, however, exhibits a rather heavy reliance on indirect taxes. Moreover, reliance on income taxes is particularly weak, amounting to only 13 percent of total taxes. Horizontal equity appears threatened because the upper decile of wage earners who pay income taxes (at progressive rates from 27 percent to 50 percent, most of which is withheld at source) seem to be taxed much more heavily than interest income and dividend earners, who, despite the "global income" concept, are taxed at a low, flat rate of 20 percent.[4] *Capital gains from financial transactions are completely untaxed.* The net result is that distributional equity is undermined; *monthly wage income* of 5 million won would be taxed at a 50 percent marginal rate, *interest income* of 5 million won would be taxed a rate of 20 percent, and 5 million won in *financial capital gains* would not be subject to any tax whatsoever.

---

3. The Final Report of the Commission on Tax Reform.

4. Although government applies a 60 percent tax rate on interest and dividend income derived from purely fictitious name accounts, because these account for only 2 percent of total transactions, it seems fair to assume that the failure to introduce the "real name" account system has seriously undermined reporting of financial transactions.

The second Achilles heel of the current tax system is the treatment of capital gains from real estate transactions, an issue related as well to the distribution of wealth. *Capital gains from real estate transactions are believed to be seriously undertaxed.* While the effective tax rate of reported capital gains in 1989 was about 25 percent, because of the disparity between market values and assessed values, the real effective rate is probably in the neighborhood of 5 to 10 percent. Given previous findings on the distribution of real estate ownership, this tax can only be described as regressive in relation to the relatively heavy burden of indirect taxes in Korea.

Various estimates of the tax burden by income decile show a relatively flat burden among upper income groups, and according to one authoritative study a secular decline over the 1970s in the tax burden on the uppermost income decile. If one were to include the interest and dividend income—which is seen in the national income accounts but is not captured in income surveys or, presumably, tax data—the effective tax rate of the top decile would be even lower. This points to the urgent need for the Office of National Tax Administration to begin collecting income-by-source statistics for all taxpayers, particularly the wealthy.

Future Policy Directions

Although greater equality in the distribution of income has been an objective of Korean tax policy during the postwar period, it has been largely overshadowed by the government's main concern for adequate revenue generation. Tax reforms in recent years, which were aimed at improving effective progressivity, have in the end yielded ad hoc increases in the tax exemptions for low-income groups. The redistributive role of the Korean tax system is undermined because, (i) the current tax system still relies heavily (although recently somewhat less extensively) on indirect taxes; (ii) most interest and dividend income is taxed separately at a low, flat tax rate; (iii) there exists no capital gains tax on financial assets; and (iv) tax authorities still apply very low property assessment values for tax purposes, although reforms are planned.

On the expenditure side of the ledger, expenditure incidence data is also sparse, so that greater efforts in studies of expenditure targeting would yield valuable new policy tools for government. This issue is well beyond the scope of this study; nevertheless, the impression formed is that the Korean government has done considerably better in alleviating absolute poverty and directing expenditures toward the lowest income groups than it has in taxing the uppermost income groups. This view is supported by the tax incidence evidence currently available in Korea, which shows very little additional progressivity in the highest income deciles. Therefore, the redistribution of income that does occur may well be from the upper-middle deciles to the lowest decile. The relative regressivity of tax payments is worsened by the underreporting of income derived from capital assets. Because it is known that the majority of these assets are held by the top decile of the income distribution, these untaxed returns to wealth are at present the major force creating greater concentration in the distribution of wealth in Korea.

Government would be well advised to focus on the relative paucity of appropriate *tax incidence data*. There is at present no statistical information on the incidence of individual taxes. Taking, for example, the reported tax revenues collected by income tax bracket, it should be possible to identify for each income group the sources of their income.[5] This kind of tax incidence data is collected in most developed countries and forms the basis of tax policy studies and tax policy assessments.[6] An official effort to upgrade data collection and analysis in the tax area should be matched by a renewed effort to survey the top income decile more extensively and ultimately to match up the two surveys to get a firmer handle on income and wealth issues.

Reforms of the tax system that attempt to reduce the reliance on indirect forms of taxation are well advised. Simplification of the global income tax schedule, particularly to remove special allowances and deductions, would also be a step in the right direction. The one reform that is overdue is legislation to bring the treatment of business income into line with income from other sources. Horizontal inequities are currently present in the way business income is reported

---

5. Global income tax data collected by the Office of National Tax Administration (ONTA) at present are not amenable to this decomposition.

6. For the United States, see Joseph A. Pechman (1985), Congressional Budget Office (1990), and Joseph A. Pechman (1990).

(although some improvement has been made recently) and by the use of a flat tax rate on interest and dividend income.

The available evidence on the underreporting of income and dividend income points to the need to reexamine the advisability of introducing "real name" accounts for financial transactions. If real name legislation is not introduced soon, there is a case for further raising the withholding tax on interest and dividends, in part to balance raised exemption levels for wages and salaries. The impact on the savings of small investors could be offset, perhaps, by allowing each adult a single savings account, with perhaps the first million won of interest tax exempt. The treatment of financial assets is only one of the concerns that currently relates to the *vertical equity* of the tax system. The second major lapse affects the treatment of land and real estate holdings.

There is little doubt that tax avoidance of capital gains on real estate has taken place in recent years, and the magnitudes involved (based on reasonable assumptions of transactions and realistic market prices) may be large. For this reason, the project being undertaken by the Ministry of Construction to revalue landholdings is an important one. Efforts should be made to coordinate the valuations for capital gains purposes with valuations used for local tax purposes. Tax rates will have to be adjusted in line with the new valuations. Before enforcement and ownership traces begin, it might be useful to institute an amnesty period for those who wish to report a previously unreported tax liability. It would also be useful to focus enforcement first in the larger and more expensive parcels and holdings. Such fundamental reforms are to be preferred to ad hoc policy measures, such as special taxes on "idle land" or edicts to force divestiture of holdings by conglomerates.

It would be a mistake to conclude that it is the tax system that is primarily to blame for the current housing situation in Korea. Clearly housing regulations, zoning requirements, the lack of personal credit markets in the form of mortgages, and the "chonsei" (lump-sum deposit rental) system are the crucial interventions in the housing sector.[7] Reforms in the housing sector and in housing finance markets

---

7. These issues are explored in a study by Kim Kyung-Hwan (1991).

in particular are long overdue. Such reforms, for example, in mortgage finance, would be complemented by consideration of tax allowances for single-family homeownership if revenue generation targets could be met by taxes on capital gains. The point worth considering is that there are prominent areas of undertaxation and significant room for increasing the progressivity of the system while at the same time addressing one fundamental social concern in Korea today—housing.

In conclusion, taxation of capital gains from financial and real assets is at present the priority in Korea. Future efforts should be directed as well at inheritance and gift taxes, which contribute little to the tax coffers and allow the intergenerational transfer of wealth to occur unimpeded. Because wealth data are in rather rudimentary form in Korea at present, and the modest efforts of this report notwithstanding, it is difficult to ascertain whether wealth is becoming more or less concentrated over time. What is clear, however, is that the distribution of wealth is significantly skewed, and that proper estimates of the gains to that wealth would substantially alter perceptions about the relative evenness of Korea's income distribution. One direct approach to retard a further deterioration of that distribution of income is to improve both horizontal and vertical equity in the tax system. The findings of this report indicate that reforms in the treatment of financial assets and capital gains from real estate, although essential for the promotion of greater horizontal equity, will also serve to strengthen the vertical equity of the system. Improvements in equity will help Korean society move into the next century with as clear a sense of national purpose and commitment to common goals as it had during the past unparalleled years of progress.

1

TRENDS IN THE DISTRIBUTION OF INCOME

Korean Income Gains

The Republic of Korea has been one of the most successful developing countries in the postwar period, whether success is measured by gains in income and consumption or by other welfare measures, such as social indicators. Rapid, export-led growth has been responsible for broadly distributed gains in real consumption and for a sharp reduction in absolute poverty. In the process, Korea has become the eleventh largest trading nation in the world economy and its per capita income level now places it close to the lower end of the spectrum of industrialized countries.

Growth of Income and Consumption

The growth of real per capita gross domestic product (GDP) in Korea can been seen in Figure 1-1 for the period from 1953 through 1985.[1] Beginning in the early 1960s, there was sustained rapid growth until the oil shock of 1979-80. The average growth rate of per capita GDP from 1963 to 1979 was a remarkable 8.1 percent. Per capita consumption did not grow quite as rapidly, because the savings and investment rates were increasing throughout this period. Nevertheless, per capita consumption grew at a rate of 6.7 percent from 1963 until 1979. It can been seen in the figure that after a brief recession, growth resumed in the early 1980s, albeit at a somewhat slower rate. The Korean economy has again grown very rapidly since 1985, adding another 15 percent to real per capita consumption between 1985 and 1989.

---

1. The data are from Summers and Heston (1988). These authors have compiled a set of estimates of real output and consumption that are comparable across countries by adjusting for differences between official exchange rates and purchasing power parities. For Korea, the data cover the period 1953-1985.

Table 1-1 provides per capita consumption figures for a number of developing and developed economies in 1963 and 1985.[2] The countries are listed in descending order of consumption level at the beginning of the period. Of this group, the developed countries had between 9.10 (U.S.) and 4.18 (Italy) times as much consumption per capita as Korea in 1963. Middle-income countries had two to three times as much. Malaysia, the Philippines, Thailand, and Taiwan, China, all had modestly more consumption for each person; only Pakistan was somewhat below Korea's level.

Figure 1-1 Per Capita GDP and Consumption, 1953-1985

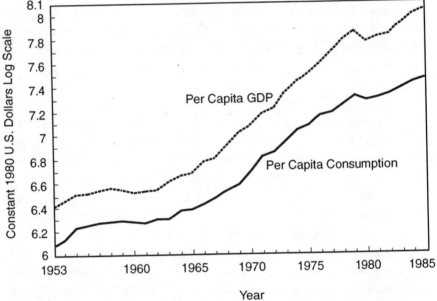

Source: Summers and Heston (1988).

---

2. The Summers and Heston data provide a good basis for comparing per capita consumption across countries. The use of per capita consumption figures for different countries compared through official exchange rates tends to be misleading, because these exchange rates generally *underestimate* real output and consumption in developing countries. The reason for this bias is that prices of nontradables, such as services, tend to be low in developing countries when compared through official exchange rates. Hence use of these exchange rates underestimates production and consumption of services in developing countries.

Table 1-1. Growth of Per Capita Consumption in Selected Economies, 1963-1985

Economy	Per capita consumption (1980 U.S.$) 1963	Per capita consumption (1980 U.S.$) 1985	Per capita consumption relative to Korea 1963	Per capita consumption relative to Korea 1985	Growth rate of per capita consumption (percent) 1963-85
United States	4,930	8,542	9.10	4.90	2.5
Australia	3,254	5,313	6.00	3.05	2.2
United Kingdom	3,227	5,174	5.95	2.97	2.1
France	3,107	6,509	5.73	3.73	3.4
Italy	2,267	4,651	4.18	2.67	3.3
Japan	1,845	4,909	3.40	2.81	4.4
Mexico	1,688	2,623	3.11	1.50	2.0
Singapore	1,602	4,430	2.96	2.54	4.6
Turkey	1,087	1,599	2.01	.92	1.8
Malaysia	794	1,649	1.46	.95	3.3
Philippines	696	1,002	1.28	.57	1.7
Taiwan, China	614	1,881	1.13	1.08	5.1
Thailand	579	1,281	1.07	.73	3.6
Korea	542	1,744	1.00	1.00	5.3
Pakistan	458	888	.85	.51	3.0

Source: Summers and Heston (1988).

Over the period examined, there has been successful growth in many of these economies. Nevertheless, it can been seen that Korea was the top performer of the group, with real per capita consumption more than tripling over the period. Annual average consumption growth has also been very impressive in Taiwan, China, at 5.1 percent, compared with 5.3 percent in Korea, as well as in Singapore, at 4.6 percent. Korea has gained substantially on other economies that have grown quite well. Its per capita consumption was below that of both Thailand and Malaysia in 1963, but by 1985 it was ahead of those economies by 36 percent and 6 percent, respectively. Per capita consumption in Korea was quite close to that of Pakistan in 1963; by

1985 the Korean level was nearly twice that of Pakistan. The consumption advantage of the developed countries over Korea was cut roughly in half over the period.

Other recognized measures of welfare gains rely on socioeconomic indicators. Korea consistently ranks very high on composite indexes such as the Physical Quality of Life Index popularized by the Overseas Development Council or the Human Development Index recently published by the United Nations Development Programme (UNDP). Equally impressive have been the gains in these welfare measures over time. Table 1-2 reports trends in selected social

Table 1-2. Trends in Social Indicators

Indicator	1970	1975	1980	1985	1989
Daily calorie supply	2,370	2,390	2,485	2,687	2,815[a]
Population per physician	1,773	1,801	1,490	1,222	1,077[a]
Population per hospital bed	1,949	1,661	1,001	549	487[a]
Population covered by health insurance (percent)	—	14.4[b]	39.3[c]	51.8	100
Enrollment ratio (percent)					
Middle school	57.0	74.2	94.6	99.7	—
High school	30.5	43.6	68.5	78.3	—
Students per teacher					
Primary school	57	52	48	38	36
Middle school	42	43	45	40	29
Housing units/number of households (percent)	78.2	74.4	74.5	69.9	70.8
Piped water supply ratio (percent)	33.2	43.1	54.6	67.2	76.0
Life expectancy	63.2	—	65.9	69.3	—
Infant mortality (per thousand live births)	39.8	—	36.8	32.6	31.0[a]

a. 1987
b. 1977
c. 1981
— Not available.
Source: Economic Planning Board, Social Indicators of Korea 1988, World Bank, Social Indicators of Development 1989.

indicators for the past two decades. Despite clear gains in health, education, and sanitation indexes, the one measure that shows scanty progress is housing. A look at the ultimate welfare indicators, such as life expectancy and infant mortality, reveals levels that are well above the average for upper-middle-income economies. There can be no doubt that gains produced over the past two decades have been tangible and broadly based.

Consumption of Housing Services

Although the overall increase in consumption has been impressive in Korea, consumption of housing services has lagged. For a typical wage-earning family, Korea's successful growth has resulted in a large increase in real purchasing power for goods and services in general. This trend can be seen in figure 1-2, which plots the average wage

Figure 1-2. Wages in Relation to Land, Housing, and Consumer Prices, 1974-1989

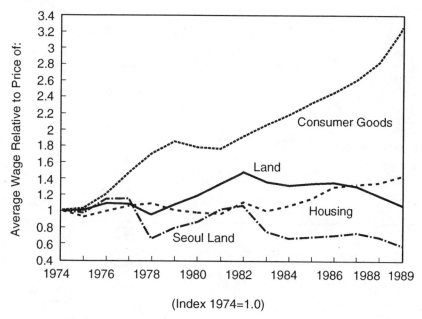

(Index 1974=1.0)

Source: Korea Housing Bank and Bank of Korea.

deflated by the consumer price index (CPI) over the period 1974-1989. Real wages *measured in housing services or land,* however, have not changed much during this time. Wages deflated by a housing price index are pretty flat over the 1974-1989 period. There has been a modest upward trend since 1984; this may be overstated by the housing price index, however, because the continuation of some price controls in the housing market makes it difficult to calculate the true rate of housing price increases (see Kim Kyung-Hwan 1991). Even if the data are taken at face value, they indicate an important difference in purchasing power for housing services, compared with purchasing power for other goods and services.

These trends in purchasing power for housing services are reflected in the data on the size of the housing stock in relation to the population. Table 1-3 shows the number of households and the

Table 1-3. Housing Stock and Number of Households

Year	Region	Population (1,000)	Number of households (A) (1,000)	Housing stock (B) (1,000)	Housing supply ratio (B/A)
1960	Korea	24,989	4,198	3,464	82.5
	Cities	6,997	1,209	783	64.8
1966	Korea	29,160	5,133	3,867	75.3
	Cities	9,805	1,838	1,160	63.1
1970	Korea	30,852	5,576	4,360	78.2
	Cities	12,685	2,404	1,398	58.2
1975	Korea	34,679	6,367	4,734	74.4
	Cities	16,770	3,216	1,809	56.3
1980	Korea	37,436	7,331	5,463	74.5
	Cities	21,441	4,294	2,542	59.2
1985	Korea	40,467	8,975	6,274	69.9
	Cities	26,458	5,937	3,428	57.7
1988	Korea	41,975	9,612	6,670	69.4
	Cities	—	6,536	3,935	60.4

— Not available.

Source: Korea Housing Bank.

number of housing units in Korea for selected years between 1960 and 1988. For Korean cities, the housing supply ratio (units divided by households) was 64.8 percent in 1960. Over the next three decades, both the housing stock and the urban population grew rapidly, with the result that the housing supply ratio for urban areas had declined modestly to 60.4 percent in 1988. For Korea as a whole, the housing supply ratio has declined substantially, from 82.5 percent in 1960 to 69.4 percent in 1988, a trend that coincides with a marked increase in urbanization. It is surprising that the supply of housing units has not kept up with growth in the number of households. There appear to be rigidities in the housing market, some of which are the result of government policies and regulations, that artificially limit the supply of this important service and maintain its price at an unnecessarily high level. The housing shortage may also have to do with the fact that land is a popular store of wealth.

Absolute and Relative Poverty

As a result of the impressive gains in income and consumption, there has been a substantial decline in absolute poverty in Korea. Table 1-4 presents some estimates of absolute poverty calculated by

Table 1-4. Trends in the Incidence of Poverty
(as a percent of total population)

Category	1965	1970	1976	1980
Absolute poverty[a]				
All households	40.9	23.4	14.8	9.8
Rural households	35.8	27.9	11.7	9.0
Urban households	54.9	16.2	18.1	10.4
Relative poverty[b]				
All households	12.1	4.8	12.4	13.3
Rural households	10.0	3.4	9.2	11.2
Urban households	17.9	7.0	16.0	15.1

a. Absolute poverty line defined as 121,000 *won* (1981 prices) a month for a five-person household.
b. Relative poverty line defined as one-third of average household income.
Source: Suh (1985).

KDI for the period 1965-1980. The poverty line for 1981 was extrapolated backward through time, controlling for general inflation, to produce the estimates. By the standards of 1981, large numbers of families were poor in 1965: 35.8 percent in rural areas and 54.9 percent in urban areas, for a (weighted) national average of 40.9 percent. The poverty rate declined steadily, to 23.4 percent of all families in 1970, 14.8 percent in 1976, and 9.8 percent in 1980. Note that by 1980 the poverty rate was similar for rural and urban sectors.

The Korea Development Institute (KDI) also calculated measures of "relative poverty." This measure is the percent of households with incomes below one-third of the average level of household income. This is another way of measuring the skewness in the income distribution. This relative measure of poverty declined dramatically from 12.1 percent in 1965 to 4.8 percent in 1970. During the 1970s, relative poverty increased, to 12.4 percent in 1976 and 13.3 percent in 1980. The trend reported in table 1-4—relative inequality declining between 1965 and 1970, then increasing between 1970 and 1976—is consistent with other information on income distribution. The magnitude of the decline between 1965 and 1970, however, seems implausible. This stability in the KDI measure of relative poverty over the whole period 1965-1980 is interesting, especially when considered in light of the steady downward trend in absolute poverty. These data suggest that changes in the *distribution of* income may not have played much of a role in reducing absolute poverty; rather, a rapid increase in *average* income appears to have been the main factor leading to a decline in poverty.[3]

---

3. That finding is consistent with the results of a recent World Bank study on poverty alleviation in Malaysia (*Malaysia: Growth, Poverty Alleviation, and Improved Income Distribution*, Report No. 8667-MA, October 1990).

Box 1. Comparing Korea's Income Distribution with that of Other Countries

In the development literature of the 1970s two assertions were frequently made concerning the household distribution of income in Korea: (1) that the distribution was relatively equitable compared with that of most developing countries; and (2) that equality had not decreased (and may have increased) during the rapid growth of the 1960s, apparently contradicting Kuznets's (1955) prediction that the distribution of income was likely to become more skewed during the early phase of industrialization.

In most comparative studies of income distribution in developing countries, Korea has been cited as an example of a country with low inequality and rapid growth. The best known of these studies is Redistribution with Growth (Chenery and others 1974). Korea in 1970 was found to be one of a small group of low-income countries characterized by low inequality. This division was done on the basis of the share of income accruing to the bottom 40 percent of the income spectrum. In Korea this share was estimated to be 18 percent; among low-income countries covered by the study, only Taiwan, China, (20.4 percent) was found to have a higher degree of equality. By comparison, the comparable figure was 13.0 percent in Tanzania (1967), 16.0 percent in India (1964), and 10.0 percent in Kenya (1969).

Korea also compared well with higher-income countries. Only a few countries in the middle-income group had greater equality than Korea. Most of the Latin American countries covered by the study had greater inequality than that found in Korea, with income shares for the bottom 40 percent of 10.0 percent in Brazil (1970), 10.5 percent in Mexico (1969), and 13.0 percent in Chile (1968). The middle-income countries found to have more equality than Korea were generally at a much higher level of development (for example, Greece and Yugoslavia). Korea even compared well with fully industrialized countries, such as Japan (20.7 percent in 1963) and the United States (19.7 percent in 1970).

Trends in Income Distribution

This section reviews trends in Korean income distribution over time. Official Economic Planning Board (EPB) estimates of income distribution have only been published since 1980, but a number of studies of Korean income distribution cover earlier periods, notably Choo and Yoon (1984) and Kim and Ahn (1987). Table 1-5 presents Gini coefficients of inequality for selected years estimated in these two studies, as well as estimates for recent years from EPB.[4] For 1988 there is also an estimate derived from a separate KDI survey of income and wealth that will be discussed at length in subsequent sections.

Table 1-5. Estimates of Gini Coefficients for Korea, Selected Years, 1965-1988

Year	EPB	Choo-Yoon	Kim-Ahn	KDI survey
1965	—	.34	.37	—
1970	—	.33	.35	—
1976	—	.39	.40	—
1980	.39	—	.39	—
1982	—	.36	.41	—
1985	.35	—	.41	—
1988	.34	—	—	.40

— Not available.
Source: Economic Planning Board, Korea Development Institute, Choo and Yoon (1984), and Kim and Ahn (1987).

---

4. The Gini coefficient is a measure of income inequality, with a higher value indicating greater inequality; the measure is based on the Lorenz curve. The Lorenz curve plots the cumulative distribution of households on the horizontal axis and the cumulative distribution of income on the vertical axis. If all households have the same income, this curve will coincide with the 45-degree line. The greater the amount of inequality, the further the curve will be beneath the 45-degree line. The Gini coefficient is the area between the 45-degree line and the Lorenz curve, divided by the total area under the 45-degree line. The Gini coefficient ranges from 0.0 (perfect equality) to 1.0 (perfect inequality, that is, all income accrues to one household).

Historical Income Distribution

The earliest firm estimates for Gini coefficients are for 1965, although even these are influenced by the quality of the data. It is encouraging that the Choo-Yoon and Kim-Ahn estimates are similar, although based on different approaches to compensate for the inherent problems of sampling bias for the very rich and the very poor. The relatively equal distribution of income witnessed in the 1965-1970 period reflects the overall poverty of the country at that time and the extensive land redistribution after the Japanese occupation. The shift to export-led development in the 1960s provided a boon to poorer agricultural households through better wage prospects in urban areas. The 1960s were characterized by a steady flow of people from the countryside to industrializing urban areas of Korea. One may speculate about why income distribution did not follow the predicted path of the Kuznet's hypothesis of worsening equity during the initial stages of growth.[5] It may well have been that the urban migrants were the poorer members of the rural population or it may reflect early interventions of government, which in 1969 began to provide higher support prices for agriculture,[6] or it may simply reflect poor sampling techniques.

During the 1970s the Choo-Yoon and Kim-Ahn estimates both indicate that income inequality increased. Choo (1985) provides some insight into the sources of this deterioration in equality by calculating income distributions for different groups in the population. Table 1-6 shows Choo's estimates for the population as a whole. Table 1-7 focuses only on agricultural households, and table 1-8 on wage/salary earners in the urban areas. It can be seen that between 1970 and 1976 there is a modest increase in the Gini coefficient for agricultural households (.29 to .33) and a somewhat greater increase for urban wage/salary earners (.30 to .36). This deterioration in equity coincides with a marked decline in the mid-1970s in the "decile distribution ratio," a comparison of the bottom and top portions of the distribution,

---

5. See Ahluwalia (1976) for a complete discussion of the Kuznets hypothesis.

6. See Moon and Kang (1986) for a chronology of agricultural intervention policies and Leipziger and Petri (1988) for comparisons of urban and rural incomes during the period.

Table 1-6. Overall Distribution of Income and Measures of Inequality
(percent)

Decile	1965	1970	1976	1982
First	1.32	2.78	1.84	2.56
Second	4.43	4.56	3.86	4.30
Third	6.47	5.81	4.93	5.46
Fourth	7.12	6.48	6.22	6.48
Fifth	7.21	7.63	7.07	7.51
Sixth	8.32	8.71	8.34	8.73
Seventh	11.32	10.24	9.91	10.03
Eighth	12.00	12.17	12.49	11.94
Ninth	16.03	16.21	17.84	14.94
Tenth	25.78	25.41	27.50	28.05
Gini coefficient	0.344	0.332	0.391	0.357
Decile distribution ratio[a]	0.463	0.472	0.372	0.437

a. Share of bottom 40 percent in relation to share of top 20 percent.
Source: Choo (1985).

Table 1-7. Distribution of Income and Measures of Inequality for Agricultural Households
(percent)

Decile	1965	1970	1976	1982
First	2.66	3.17	2.46	2.75
Second	6.39	5.19	4.32	4.82
Third	6.67	6.00	6.05	6.06
Fourth	6.91	6.88	6.62	7.18
Fifth	7.16	8.10	7.81	8.24
Sixth	9.63	9.01	9.13	9.40
Seventh	10.83	10.59	10.48	10.78
Eighth	11.73	12.42	12.51	12.47
Ninth	15.61	17.87	16.79	15.02
Tenth	22.42	20.77	23.83	23.28
Gini coefficient	0.285	0.295	0.327	0.306
Decile distribution ratio[a]	0.593	0.550	0.479	0.543

a. Share of bottom 40 percent in relation to share of top 20 percent.
Source: Choo (1985).

and a significant increase in overall poverty as seen in table 1-6. This is consistent with the data reported in table 1-8, which shows large reductions in the income share of the lowest employee households as well as employer households.

The most interesting result concerns the Gini coefficient for the self-employed and employer households (table 1-9), which increases from .35 in 1970 to .45 in 1976. Not only does the self-employed/employer group show the largest increase in inequality, but it also has the highest level of inequality. The latter fact is important, because this is a group that increased in relative size throughout the 1970s. These results seem to indicate that during the 1970s a substantial urban, high-income group developed, composed of professionals, managers, and owners of capital, and that this development resulted in an overall deterioration in the income

Table 1-8. Distribution of Income and Measures of Inequality for Employee Households
(percent)

Decile	1965	1970	1976	1982
First	0.28	2.59	2.08	3.22
Second	1.90	5.39	4.50	4.97
Third	5.31	6.32	5.53	6.03
Fourth	7.00	6.46	6.40	6.94
Fifth	7.68	8.85	7.50	7.93
Sixth	9.72	8.94	8.59	9.04
Seventh	11.00	10.16	10.15	10.37
Eighth	13.32	12.19	11.89	12.12
Ninth	16.67	14.84	15.48	14.96
Tenth	27.13	24.26	27.87	24.42
Gini coefficient	0.399	0.304	0.355	0.309
Decile distribution ratio[a]	0.331	0.536	0.347	0.537

a. Share of bottom 40 percent in relation to share of top 20 percent.
Source: Choo (1985).

distribution.[7] This is one of the potential sources of growing inequality noted by Kuznets. If the ownership of agricultural land is fairly equitable, then it is likely that income distribution within the urban/industrial sector will be more skewed than in the agricultural sector. This is because the assets in the industrial sector, such as the physical capital stock and specialized skills, are not likely to be owned in an equitable manner, at least in the early stages of development. The expansion of the industrial sector, in relation to the agricultural sector, can then generate increased overall inequality.

Table 1-9. Distribution of Income and Measures of Inequality for Employer Households
(percent)

Decile	1965	1970	1976	1982
First	2.24	2.58	1.15	1.75
Second	3.44	4.06	2.41	3.25
Third	4.06	4.59	3.36	4.22
Fourth	5.48	6.39	4.43	5.40
Fifth	6.93	6.96	6.01	6.50
Sixth	8.85	9.26	7.79	7.89
Seventh	10.44	10.59	9.91	9.31
Eighth	15.47	13.55	16.57	11.63
Ninth	17.95	18.01	22.27	15.17
Tenth	25.14	24.02	26.11	34.88
Gini coefficient	0.384	0.353	0.449	0.445
Decile distribution ratio[a]	0.360	0.419	0.235	0.292

a. Share of bottom 40 percent in relation to share of top 20 percent.
Source: Choo (1985).

This may appear to contradict the earlier explanation of why income distribution apparently improved in the 1960s. If the within-sector inequality is high in industry and if industry has been

---

7. This is the period of Heavy and Chemical Industry (HCI) preferences, during which government intervention in the allocation of scarce capital was extensive (see World Bank 1987).

expanding in relation to agriculture throughout 1960-80, then why has income distribution not deteriorated continuously? A potential answer to this question lies in the changing relative importance of industry and agriculture. In the early 1960s industry was small in Korea; in 1964, for example, only 8.8 percent of the labor force was in industry, while 29.3 percent was in services and 61.9 percent in agriculture (see figure 1-3). If the industrial sector is small, inequality within that sector may not have much effect on the overall distribution of income. If the shifting of surplus labor out of agriculture reduces income inequality among the households that remain in the sector and reduces disparity between the agricultural and industrial sectors, then overall equity could be improved.

Figure 1-3. Structure of GDP and Employment, 1964-1989

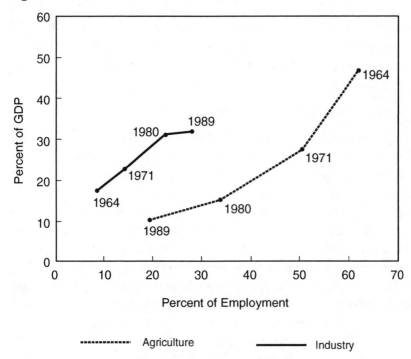

Source: Bank of Korea.

As the pool of surplus labor dwindles and eventually is eliminated, however, this process comes to an end. Furthermore, as the urban/industrial sector grows, inequality within that sector has more and more influence upon the overall distribution of income. By 1980 the share of labor in the agricultural sector had declined to 34.0 percent, while shares in industry and services had increased, to 22.5 percent and 43.5 percent, respectively.

It appears that as long as there was surplus labor in the agricultural sector that could be absorbed into urban employment, Korea was able to avoid the deterioration in income distribution predicted by Kuznets. Once surplus labor had been absorbed (around 1970), further expansion of industry in relation to agriculture resulted in the predictable decline of equity. The changing trend in the distribution of income may have been accelerated by the shift in industrial policy away from neutral export promotion to targeted development of capital-intensive industries under the Heavy and Chemical Industry (HCI) program. That program channeled low-cost loans to a small number of large firms. It probably accelerated industrial development, but it also concentrated the ownership of industrial assets in the hands of a few families.

Income Distribution in the 1980s

There is widespread agreement that income distribution in Korea improved during the 1960s and deteriorated in the 1970s, although the specific numbers are subject to debate. What has happened to income distribution in the 1980s is a matter of considerable controversy. The statistical basis for the construction of income distribution estimates has improved in the 1980s as no group was deliberately excluded, although subject to the caveats related to coverage noted in the subsequent section on data problems.

Table 1-10 presents the income distribution by decile, as calculated from the EPB surveys of 1980, 1985, and 1988. For the country as a whole, these data show a marked improvement in equality between 1980 and 1985. The share of income accruing to the bottom 20 percent, for instance, increased from 5.09 percent in 1980 to 6.96 percent in 1985, whereas the share of the top quintile declined from

Table 1-10. Distribution of Income and Measures of Inequality in the 1980s

Income decile	National			Urban			Rural		
	1980	1985	1988	1980	1985	1988	1980	1985	1988
First	1.57	2.59	2.81	1.46	2.26	2.80	1.76	3.18	2.93
Second	3.52	4.37	4.58	3.31	4.05	4.46	3.88	4.91	4.99
Third	4.86	5.48	5.65	4.65	5.21	5.47	5.29	6.04	6.19
Fourth	6.11	6.47	6.64	5.87	6.16	6.39	6.55	7.05	7.28
Fifth	7.33	7.57	7.60	7.12	7.25	7.35	7.83	8.12	8.38
Sixth	8.63	8.73	8.67	8.40	8.48	8.43	9.13	9.32	9.47
Seventh	10.21	10.10	10.01	10.07	9.92	9.79	10.66	10.55	10.74
Eighth	12.38	11.97	11.80	12.23	11.94	11.64	12.71	12.28	12.47
Ninth	15.93	15.10	14.62	16.09	15.33	14.58	15.98	14.96	14.99
Tenth	29.46	27.62	27.62	30.80	29.40	29.09	26.21	23.59	22.56
Gini coefficient	0.389	0.345	0.336	0.405	0.369	0.350	0.356	0.297	0.290

Source: Economic Planning Board.

45.39 percent to 42.72 percent. The ratio of the top quintile's income to that of the bottom quintile was nearly 9:1 in 1980, falling to around 6:1 in 1985. One thing to keep in mind was that 1980 was a recession year, so that these data may reflect cyclical factors as well as secular trends. Between 1985 and 1988 the income distribution calculated from the EPB surveys was stable.

Trends within urban and rural sectors followed the overall direction closely. In both sectors, income shares of the bottom quintile increased between 1980 and 1985, while the share of the top quintile declined. It remained true throughout this period that inequality was somewhat greater in the urban sector than in the rural areas. For example, the bottom 20 percent of households in urban areas earned 6.31 percent of urban income in 1985; the bottom 20 percent of rural households had 8.09 percent of rural income.

Other studies of income distribution in the 1980s present a somewhat different picture, however. The Gini coefficients calculated from the EPB surveys show a decline from .39 in 1980 to .34 in 1985 and 1988. The Kim-Ahn study, however, finds that the Gini coefficient increased modestly from .39 in 1980 to .41 in 1982 and 1985 (table 1-5). The KDI survey of household income in 1988 similarly indicates a Gini coefficient of .40. Thus, the available evidence on changing distribution of income in the 1980s is inconclusive. None of the studies, however, shows any large increase in inequality.

According to other conventional measures, income distribution has improved slightly in the 1980s. Labor's income share in national income increased from 51.9 percent in 1980 to 53.2 percent in 1985 and to 54.2 percent in 1988. The share of the bottom 40 percent in total income also improved from 16.1 percent in 1980 to 18.9 percent in 1985 and to 19.7 percent in 1988. Nevertheless, a public perception exists that the income distribution may have become more concentrated toward the highest income group because of skyrocketing returns on asset holdings, especially land. (This will be addressed in the section on distribution of landholdings in chapter 2.)

Recent Evidence and Issues

Problems with the Data Base

One of the reasons why it is difficult to resolve the debates about Korean income distribution is that there are some serious problems with the underlying data base. Beginning in 1963 the Korean government has carried out separate annual income surveys of city and farm households. Until 1977 the urban survey deliberately excluded households on public assistance (that is, those who were legally "low-income class"), as well as households with income above a certain level. Thus the low end and the high end of the income spectrum were omitted from the surveys. These exclusions were ended in 1977, so that the data base for the 1980s is considerably improved.

The urban survey, however, does not include income data for self-employed and employer households; only expenditure data is reported for these groups. Furthermore, it remains true that rural, nonagricultural households are not covered by the annual surveys. These remaining exclusions are serious. Table 1-11 lists the excluded categories and the share of total households that they represent, according to the 1980 population census. The urban self-employed

Table 1-11. Uncovered Households in the CHIES and FHES Surveys

Category	Number of households (1,000)	Percent of all households
Urban self-employed	1,628	20.4
Non-farm in rural area	1,307	16.4
Wage and salary earning	(835)	(10.5)
Self-employed	(472)	(5.9)
Fishery	157	2.0
Small farm and wage-earning in rural area	42	0.5
Total	3,134	39.3

Source: Choo and Yoon (1984), p. 4 (based on *Housing and Population Census*, 1980).

and employer households make up 20.4 percent of all households, whereas the nonfarm households in rural areas account for 16.4 percent of all households. (Two minor additional groups are excluded from coverage: fishery households and small-farm households.) *Therefore, roughly two-fifths of all households have been excluded from the coverage of the annual income surveys.*

Income distribution estimates based on these annual surveys thus require quite a few critical assumptions. The self-employed and employer households in urban areas include many of the richest families, as well as owners of small retail outlets who might be in the middle or low end of the income distribution. The usual approach in calculating Korean income distribution estimates is to use the figures on household *expenditures* for these groups to estimate their household income. This requires strong assumptions about the nature and stability of the relationship between expenditure and income, as well as confidence that the expenditure data are accurate. Furthermore, assumptions must be made about the income of nonfarm rural households.

Calculations of income distribution before 1977 face the additional problem that the urban poor and urban rich were deliberately excluded from coverage. Korean researchers were aware of this problem and tried to modify the original survey data.[8] The common approach has been to attempt to estimate the income of the rich households from tax data; however, there is some doubt about the accuracy of the income figures in the tax data, because underreporting of income was and continues to be a serious problem.

Problems with the data base leave room for debate about income distribution in Korea, and there have been some reexaminations that attempt to show that the distribution in Korea is not as equitable as first thought.[9] The most interesting finding that evolves from these adjustments is that Bhalla (1979) estimates the income share accruing to the top two deciles of the distribution at between 49 percent and 52 percent, compared with the 45 percent reported in table 1-6, using official data. *Clearly the greatest potential inaccuracy in the income distribution data is in the upper tail of the distribution.*

The KDI Survey for 1988

KDI conducted its own national household survey of income and wealth for 1988, although on a smaller scale than the government's surveys, which is an important new piece of evidence about the current status of income and wealth distribution in Korea. The survey is unique because it covers both income and wealth.[10] The results of that survey concerning wealth will be presented in the next chapter. This section will briefly review the findings regarding income distribution.

Table 1-12 presents the household distribution of income by kind of income for 1988. Decile shares are shown and further reported in the appendix to this chapter, where a basic reconciliation between the

---

8. Choo and Yoon (1984) and Kim and Ahn (1987).

9. Bhalla (1979), for example, calculated a range of estimates for income distribution in 1976 by examining the impact of different assumptions about the groups excluded from the household surveys. Bhalla's adjustments for 1976 yield a smaller share (by perhaps 1 percent) for the lowest 20 percent of the population, a marginally lower share for the bottom 40 percent, and a rather significantly higher share for the top 20 percent of the distribution, approximately 5 percent higher than Choo's reported results in table 1-5 for the same year.

10. It should be noted that as with most surveys the KDI survey is not without its critics: its sample size is said to be small compared with EPB sample size and in many cases own consumption of farm households was omitted in reporting income because it was not done by the household bookkeeping method.

Table 1-12. Household Distribution of Income by Category, 1988 (thousand won)

Income decile	Total income	Income shares (percent)	Wage and salaries	Surplus from self-employed		Property income			Transfer income	Others	Capital gains
				Total	Farming	Total	Rents	Dividends & interest			
1	85	(1.2)	9	49	40	6	5	1	12	7	2
2	243	(3.3)	58	142	82	13	11	2	16	13	0
3	327	(4.5)	164	123	65	13	9	4	16	16	0
4	427	(5.9)	259	119	80	16	12	4	16	16	1
5	532	(7.4)	349	129	69	19	13	6	18	16	1
6	625	(8.6)	236	359	38	16	11	5	4	8	2
7	728	(10.0)	489	180	64	32	25	7	11	13	2
8	898	(12.4)	574	225	83	51	34	17	26	15	7
9	1,128	(15.6)	564	470	79	60	47	13	18	10	6
10	2,250	(31.1)	845	984	97	221	156	65	49	30	121
Average	724.3	(100.0)	354.7	278.0	69.7	44.7	32.3	12.4	18.6	14.4	14.2

Source: Korea Development Institute (1989).

KDI survey and national income accounts data is performed. It is important to note that the KDI survey finds considerably more income inequality than the EPB estimates for the same year (table 1-10). For example, EPB estimates the income share of the bottom 40 percent to be 19.68 percent, whereas the lowest 40 percent in the KDI survey accounts for only 14.93 percent of total household income. This 5 percentage point difference is substantial. The top 20 percent of households received 42.34 percent of income according to EPB, but garnered 46.63 percent of the income covered by the KDI survey.

It is not surprising that surveys would yield somewhat different estimates, because income distribution data collected from sample surveys are exposed to a number of errors. Households may refuse to supply the information requested, and if this nonresponse is related to income, the overall results will be biased. Similar problems arise if individuals under- (or over-) report receipts from different sources. Reliability will also be influenced by the size of the sample. A common method of assessing the overall reliability of income data derived from surveys is to compare the aggregate figures reported for components of income with independent estimates obtained from the national accounts. An attempt has been made to perform such an exercise in the context of disaggregated income data provided by the KDI in table 1-13.

Column 1 of table 1-13 reports the overall average monthly receipts for various components of income obtained from the KDI survey. Column 3 of table 1-13 reports the 1988 national accounts figure which most closely matches the KDI category. A comparison of the KDI and national accounts figures provides grounds for some degree of confidence in the KDI data. The aggregate income estimate of 89,473 billion won is only 13 percent short of personal sector income, and some of this discrepancy may be readily explained. For example, individuals may well report their wages and salaries net of direct taxes and social security contributions (respectively, 4,271 billion won and 2,039 billion won in 1988). The relatively low national accounts value for rent, and the correspondingly high figure for "other transfers" probably reflects in part the way that "Chonsei deposits" are treated in the national accounts. It may also be the case that some of the interhousehold transfers recorded under "other transfers" are not viewed as income by the households concerned.

Table 1-13. Comparison of KDI Income Figures with National Accounts, 1988

	KDI			BOK
KDI survey component	Average monthly income (thousand won)	Aggregate annual income[a] (billion won)	National income (billion won)	National income component
Wage & salaries	354.7	44,692	53,197	Compensation of employees
Surplus from				Operating surplus and
self-employed	278.0	35,028	31,762	entrepreneurial income
Farming	(69.7)	(8,782)	(11,240)	Agriculture, forestry, fishing
Property income	44.7	5,632	6,318	Property income
Rents	(32.3)	(4,070)	(771)	Rent
Interest and dividends	(12.4)	(1,562)	(5,547)	Interest & dividends
Transfer income	18.6	2,344	2,058	Social security benefits & social assistance grants
Other income	14.4	1,814	9,588	Other transfers
Total income (excluding capital gains)	710.1	89,473	102,923	Total receipts (excluding insurance claims)

a. Obtained by multiplying average monthly income by 12 (months) x 10.5 (million households).
Source: Bank of Korea (1990).

The most worrying aspect of the survey data appears to be the very low amount reported for interest and dividends, which is barely one-quarter of the national accounts figure. There seems no obvious explanation for this apart from a low response rate and underreporting by the more affluent households. As discussed in chapter 2, it is fairly clear that the greatest underreporting of wealth holdings occurs in the top one percent of the wealth distribution. As is also extensively discussed, the returns to wealth holding in Korea have been extremely large in recent years, although official statistics do not capture this phenomenon adequately.

Linkages between Distributions of Income and Wealth

As noted, the evidence concerning trends in the distribution of income in the 1980s is inconclusive. The EPB figures show diminished inequality, whereas other data indicate no significant change. There are no data, however, suggesting that income distribution has actually worsened in the 1980s. Nevertheless, the public perception that income distribution is becoming more skewed is very strong. One possible explanation of the variance between public perception and the results of income distribution studies is that there are inequities associated with the *distribution of wealth* in Korea that are not well reflected in household surveys of income.

In general, there is a close connection between the distribution of income and the distribution of wealth. As a rough rule, about three-quarters of national income is a return to labor, while the remaining quarter is a return to capital (including land). It is difficult to say how well Korea conforms to this norm, because the national income accounts do not clearly divide factor income into labor compensation and property income. In the Korean accounts for 1988, 54 percent of domestic factor income is clearly labor compensation. The remaining 46 percent is "operating surplus" of incorporated and unincorporated entities, including farm income. In industry and certain services (for example, finance, real estate, and insurance), virtually all of this surplus is a return to land and capital. In agriculture, retail trade, and restaurants, much of the operating surplus is a return to labor. On the assumption that 100 percent of operating surplus is a return to property in the former class of industries, and that 75 percent of operating surplus is a return to labor in the latter group, property income as a whole would be about 30 percent of total factor income in

Korea. The distribution of this 30 percent of total income depends on the distribution of the tangible wealth that creates this flow.

The income accruing to property may not be well captured in household income surveys for several reasons. As noted in the previous section, the KDI household survey seemed to suffer from underreporting of interest and dividend payments. More important, much of what is property income from the standpoint of the national accounts is not received as money income by households. For instance, much of corporate earnings are retained for reinvestment, rather than distributed to shareholders. These corporate retained earnings are included in the national accounts as property income, but no household receives a direct payment corresponding to this income. Rather, retained earnings are one of the important foundations for increases in the value of corporate securities held by shareholders. Shareholders receive the income from retained earnings only when they sell their shares and realize capital gains. As long as shareholders hold their securities, an important part of their property income is not realized and hence cannot be captured even in the most accurate of household income surveys.

There are similar problems with treatment of income from land. In principle, the national accounts should include not just land rentals actually paid, but also the *implicit rental value of properties occupied by the owner*. In particular, the implicit rental value of owner-occupied housing should be a significant figure in the national accounts, forming one of the components of property income. In a household income survey, however, "real income" that is not monetized will not be counted.

The general point is that the distribution of land, housing, corporate securities, and other forms of marketable wealth has a significant impact on the distribution of real income, in the most basic sense of consumption of goods and services. Income from wealth will only be reflected in income distribution data calculated from household surveys in a very limited way. To the extent that some wealth generates annual income in the form of rent, interest, or dividends, its impact will be reflected in a good household survey. Furthermore, if household surveys suffer from underreporting of such property income, it is possible to correct for this deficiency with ad hoc adjustments.

A very preliminary attempt is made in the calculations underlying table 1-14 to factor in investment income as well as realized capital gains to ascertain, even illustratively, whether this inclusion materially alters the income distribution picture in Korea. This kind of analysis is provided as a template for further work by Korean researchers and as a guide to policymakers interested in linking wealth and income issues more explicitly. The underlying assumption needed at present to reconcile income and wealth distributions is that earned income and investment income are highly correlated, at least by decile.[11] The starting point is earnings shares. Adjustments have been applied to earnings shares, based on national income figures, to account for own employment income more fully.[12] Earnings shares by decile are not markedly different from the income shares of the 1988 KDI survey. Two significant further adjustments are made to illustrate the potential impact of unreported asset earnings. The first adjustment uses the constructed wealth distribution of chapter 2 to generate an investment income flow by decile.[13] The second adjustment adds in a modest amount of capital gains (equal to 10 percent) as realized income derived from real assets that are sold. As can be seen from the adjusted Lorenz curves, the distribution of income becomes significantly more skewed in figure 1-4 once these indicative income adjustments have been included.

---

11. This is clearly not a perfect assumption because income shares in the bottom half of the distribution will exceed investment income shares. Because most wealth is concentrated in the uppermost decile, and wealth is more concentrated than income, such an assumption will still underestimate the effect of investment income on income distribution. It would be analytically preferable to be able to match the income and wealth distributions with precision.

12. Earnings shares are calculated by taking wages and salaries from national income as reported in table 1-13, assuming that half of self-employed income is earnings, and including transfer and other income.

13. Investment income by decile is derived from the wealth distribution shown on table 2-13 (adjustment B) and reported in Appendix 2.3. Total wealth is taken to be 717.1 trillion won as reported in table 2-11. A one-to-one correspondence between income and wealth deciles is assumed for purposes of the exercise.

Table 1-14. Estimated Wealth Adjusted Income Data
(percent)

Income decile	Earnings shares	Earnings + investment income shares	Earnings + investment income + capital gains
1	1.0	0.7	0.6
2	3.0	2.1	1.8
3	4.9	3.5	3.1
4	6.7	5.0	4.4
5	8.5	6.6	5.9
6	8.1	7.1	6.8
7	11.4	9.9	9.3
8	13.8	12.4	11.9
9	15.7	15.6	15.5
10	26.9	37.1	40.7

Source: Staff estimates for 1988, in part based on wealth shares as reported in Kwon (1990) adjusted according to table 2-13.

These adjustments can be proposed for any distribution of income and are of heuristic value in showing the effect of unreported or underreported income. Gini coefficients are deliberately not calculated. It is important to note that when wealth generates income in other forms, such as direct consumption of housing services or unrealized but collaterable capital gains, its importance will not be accurately captured in household survey data, even after such adjustments. What is useful, however, is to try and begin to link the distribution of wealth, and the income and capital gains derived from it, to the distribution of income. This link, it is argued, reveals a lot about the underlying tensions in Korean society that have emerged in the last decade. For this reason it is necessary to supplement the analysis of income distribution with studies that look directly at the distribution of wealth. The next chapter examines the evidence on the distribution of wealth in Korea and considers the implications of that distribution.

Figure 1-4. Illustrative Wealth-Adjusted Lorenz Curve

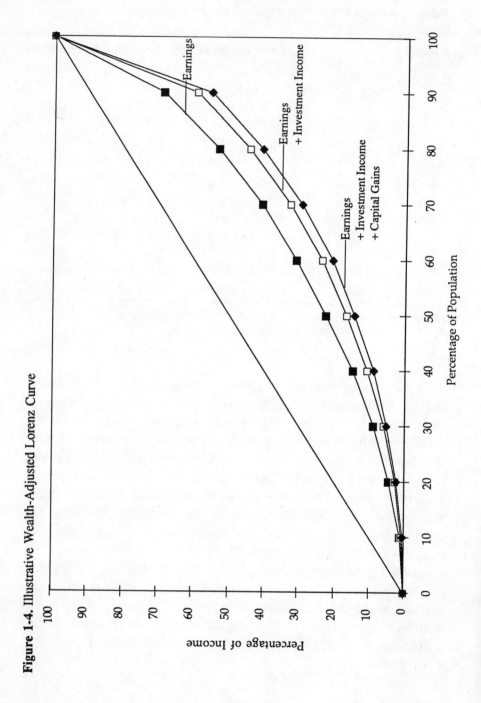

Development Lessons

Three general lessons emerge from this review of developments in Korea's distribution of income. First, no evidence is found that, based on generally accepted measures of income distribution, rapid industrialization has led to a deterioration in income distribution. Second, there is ample evidence that a strong human capital base in rural areas in particular is necessary for industrial transformation to take place smoothly; that is, to enfranchise the poor. Finally, rapid growth, based on labor-intensive industrialization, is likely to be the most effective means of eradicating absolute poverty, with more impact than alternative programs specifically targeted to fight poverty.

Concerning the first general lesson, Kuznets formulated his hypothesis that the distribution of income would worsen during the early stages of industrialization on the basis of the historical experience of early industrializers like the United Kingdom and the United States. It is now clear that this is not a general proposition, and it is not necessarily applicable to late developers. In the early developers, industrialization was based primarily on the domestic market and involved the simultaneous expansion of consumer goods industries and producer goods industries like metal and machinery. One of the distinguishing features of the late developers is that their industrialization is much more dependent on exports. This pattern of development enables production to remain concentrated in relatively labor-intensive consumer goods sectors for a considerable period of time before the heavy industrial sectors need to be developed. An export-oriented development strategy thus facilitates the rapid absorption of surplus labor from rural areas into manufacturing production. As evidenced by Korea's experience in the 1960s, the effect of this expansion on the distribution of income is likely to have been neutral or better.

The policy basis for Korea's success should not be oversimplified, however. A second general lesson that can be drawn from the Korean experience is that the rapid shift of labor from low-productivity rural occupations to higher-productivity urban and industrial activities was facilitated by a strong human capital base. In particular, the relatively equal distribution of land in the 1950s in Korea meant that there were few pockets of extreme poverty and malnutrition. Furthermore, rural education was highly developed so that children acquired the skills and knowledge relevant to modern sector employment. It would be difficult if not impossible to replicate Korea's experience in developing countries where significant portions of the rural population suffer from malnutrition, disease, and poor education. Such countries would have to address these rural problems through measures such as land redistribution and improvements in rural health and education before they could expect to get the same kind of results from export-oriented trade policies.

A final general point of extreme importance is that increases in per capita income are likely to be the most important means of reducing poverty. In Korea, while there remains debate about the details of trends in distributional measures such as the Gini coefficient, it is clear that between 1960 and 1980 there was no large shift in the distribution of income in either direction. Yet the incidence of poverty declined substantially, because real income rose dramatically for all segments of the income spectrum. The way in which the pie was divided among different groups remained fairly stable, but the size of the pie grew enormously.

These three general lessons are likely to be applicable to newly industrializing developing countries, even those at the lowest stage of development. There are other features of the Korean experience that raise interesting questions for the small group of rapidly growing countries that are closing in on the developed world. After relying for more than a decade on labor-intensive exports to be the engine of growth, the Korean government in the late 1970s adopted a targeted policy of building up heavy industries. There remains considerable debate about the wisdom of this strategy as an industrial policy, but there has been little examination of the effect of the policy on the distribution of income and wealth. The available information of the distribution of income is not sufficiently sensitive to these shifts in industrial policy. Even though available evidence may not show large shifts in equity, there is collateral evidence that the owners of capital in preferred sectors gained large rents from heavily subsidized credits. This may have had long-lasting effects in the creation of wealth, as described in the following chapter.

Appendix 1-1: Reconciliation of KDI and National Accounts Data

To assess the effect that underreporting might have on the income distribution data, a number of adjustments have been made to the KDI estimates of decile shares. The first and second columns of table 1-15 give the figures computed directly from the KDI data. The third and fourth columns recalculate these figures when capital gains are removed from the definition of income. The data are then made consistent with the national accounts by scaling each of the income components up or down until the aggregate figure matches that in the national accounts. Thus, for example, wages and salaries are all scaled up by the factor $44692/53197 = 1.19$. In the case of rental income, it has been assumed that the KDI survey figure is correct, and the "other transfers" category in the national accounts has accordingly been reduced to $9588-(4070-771) = 6289$. The recomputed decile shares are recorded in the sixth column.

The results of this exercise indicate that omitting capital gains from the definition of income leads to a small rise in the shares of all income groups apart from the top decile, as would be expected from the very high concentration of capital gains in the richest group. Scaling the income components so that they conform with the national accounts figures raises the average monthly income by 15 percent, but has little impact on the decile shares, except for a redistribution of 1 percent of total income away from the top 20 percent of the population. The close correspondence between the second and sixth columns suggests that the decile shares derived from the KDI survey are not significantly affected by either the removal of capital gains or underreporting of income components.

This validation procedure is not completely comprehensive because it does not allow for differential response rates by income level. Furthermore, the reconciliation with national accounts should in principle be undertaken with individual survey returns. Simply recomputing the income receipts of each income decile does not take into account the reranking of individuals that would take place at the micro level. Because this reranking would tend to raise the shares of the top groups and lower the shares of the bottom groups, there are further grounds for confidence in the decile shares computed by KDI as a basic approximation of the real distribution by decile.

Table 1-15. Reconciliation of KDI Survey Data with National Accounts

Income decile	Original KDI figures		KDI figures less capital gains		KDI components reconciled with national accounts	
	Monthly income (thousand won)	Income share (%)	Monthly income (thousand won)	Income share (%)	Monthly income (thousand won)	Income share (%)
1	85	1.2	83	1.2	99	1.2
2	243	3.3	242	3.4	275	3.4
3	327	4.5	332	4.7	400	4.9
4	427	5.9	426	6.0	512	6.3
5	532	7.4	531	7.5	638	7.8
6	625	8.6	623	8.8	666	8.2
7	728	10.0	725	10.2	850	10.4
8	898	12.4	891	12.5	1,056	12.9
9	1,128	15.6	1,122	15.8	1,241	15.2
10	2,250	31.1	2,129	30.0	2,432	29.8
Average	724.3		710.4		816.7	
Total		100.0		100.0		100.0

2

THE DISTRIBUTION OF WEALTH IN KOREA

It is notoriously difficult to collect information on holdings of personal wealth. In no country in the world does the quality of data or personal wealth match the quality of the principal economic indicators or even of data on the distribution of income. The most reliable information is found in tax records in countries that tax individuals' wealth, using a comprehensive coverage of assets, but few countries do so. For other countries, estimates of the distribution of wealth are derived indirectly from sample surveys, property tax returns, inheritance tax records, data on investment income, and other publicly available documents, such as registers of shareholdings. Each of these data sources is potentially available for Korea, but not always in a form that is easy to exploit—and they all have limitations. Data on inheritances, for example, cover only a minority of the population, and sample surveys suffer more from nonresponse and undervaluation than other types of economic data. Checks and adjustments can be made to assess the reliability and improve the quality of data, but statistics on the distribution of wealth should always be viewed with skepticism.

Moreover, inequality of wealth may be calculated in different ways. Estimates can be provided for different economic units (individuals or families) using various definitions of "wealth" and employing alternative methods of valuation. Gross personal wealth includes any asset an individual owns, or partly owns, and from the sale of which he or she would be entitled to share in the proceeds. This includes holdings of real assets (land, buildings, and other property; business assets; and household goods such as furniture, consumer durables, and automobiles) as well as financial assets (such as cash, savings accounts, government bonds, and corporate stock).[1] Personal wealth can also be

---

1. The appropriate price for an asset depends on the valuation convention adopted. Assets are normally assigned the price they could be expected to fetch if sold on the open market (the "sell-up value"). But this price may be considerably less than

defined to include items that yield a capital sum, or a stream of income, but that are not readily marketable—for example, insurance policies, pension rights, and human capital (the expected present value of future earnings). No attempt is made here to cover pension rights or human capital, but, where possible, the value of insurance policies will be treated as a component of gross personal wealth. Net personal wealth is taken to represent gross personal wealth less debts.

Assessing the distribution of personal wealth in Korea poses special problems because most sources cover only a subset of data on personal wealth, such as financial assets or land—with the single exception of a 1988 survey conducted by the Korea Development Institute (KDI). Despite the dearth of comprehensive data, combining evidence from several sources yields a reasonably accurate estimate of the overall inequality of wealth. In light of the pressures on government to deal with the perceived issue of increasing inequality and the political objectives of the Seventh Five Year Plan to bring about a greater equality in the distribution of income, independent assessments of the distribution of wealth are a useful source of information to policymakers.

Surveys of Wealth Holdings in Korea

The KDI Survey

In a 1988 survey of the income and wealth of a nationally representative sample of 4,291 households (see Kwon 1990), KDI found that more than 90 percent of Korea's gross personal wealth is held in the form of real assets, and that 40 percent of households claim to have virtually no savings or financial assets of any kind (see table 2-1). The distribution of financial assets is more unequal than the distribution of real assets, which are in turn more unequally distributed

---

the asset's value as a "going concern" to the current owner. The distinction between the "sell-up" and "going concern" price is particularly important in the valuation of household goods and unincorporated businesses. It can also be significant in valuing major shareholdings in corporations, where the quoted share price may not be appropriate for large blocks of shares. For further details on the problems of estimating the distribution of personal wealth, see Atkinson and Harrison (1978a, b).

Table 2-1. The Distribution of Household Income and Wealth in Korea, 1988

Decile	Gross personal wealth		Financial assets		Real assets		
	Average holding (million won)	Share (%)	Average holding (million won)	Share (%)	Average holding (million won)	Share (%)	Income share (%)
1	2.6	0.5	0	0	1.4	0.3	1.4
2	7.2	1.3	0	0	5.3	1.0	3.5
3	12.4	2.2	0	0	9.9	1.9	4.6
4	18.8	3.4	0.0	0.1	16.2	3.2	6.1
5	27.2	4.9	0.7	1.6	23.8	4.6	7.5
6	37.1	6.6	1.7	3.6	33.8	6.6	8.7
7	50.4	9.0	2.7	5.8	45.9	9.0	10.1
8	67.4	12.0	4.7	10.1	62.1	12.1	12.5
9	95.3	17.0	8.1	17.4	88.3	17.2	15.6
10	240.9	43.1	28.6	61.4	225.9	44.1	29.9
All groups	55.9	100.0	4.7	100.0	51.3	100.0	100.0
Gini coefficient		0.58		0.77		0.60	0.40

Source: Kwon (1990).

than gross personal wealth. The top 20 percent of households, for instance, are reported to own 60.1 percent of gross personal wealth, but 61.3 percent of real assets and 78.8 percent of financial assets. As in other countries, wealth in Korea is considerably more unequal than income: the 23.1 percent share of total income received by the bottom half of the income distribution is almost double the 12.3 percent share of personal wealth owned by the bottom half of the wealth distribution. Compare also the Gini inequality value of 0.40 for income with 0.58 for gross personal wealth and 0.77 for financial assets.

In Korea, 43.1 percent of the wealth is in the hands of the top 10 percent of households, 30.1 percent is in the hands of the top 5 percent, and 14.2 percent in the hands on the top 1 percent, according to KDI data. These statistics were estimated by assuming that the top tail of income and wealth distributions can be successfully approximated by the Pareto distribution: $N(w) = Bw^{-A}$, where N(w) denotes the number of people with wealth greater than w, and A is the Pareto coefficient.[2]

The distribution of personal wealth in Korea is not exceptionally out of line compared with several developed countries a decade or two ago (see table 2-2). Indeed, the shares of wealth for the top 10 percent and 20 percent of Koreans are lower than in all countries on table 2-2 except Australia. Comparing household survey data for Korea with similar data for Australia, Canada, France, and Sweden, it appears that Korea most resembles France in about 1975—roughly midway between the low degree of inequality in Australia and the high degree in Canada and Sweden.

Many of the figures in table 2-2 refer to the distribution of wealth among individuals rather than households, and are estimated from estate tax returns rather than sample surveys. Where both household and individual estimates are available for a country and are calculated from both survey and tax data, as for France and Australia, the distribution of wealth is more unequal across individuals than across households. Several other factors are relevant in comparing the evidence for Korea with other countries. First, the comparative data are generally fifteen to twenty years old, and inequality of wealth in developed countries has been declining for fifty years or more.[3] Therefore,

---

2. The Pareto distribution provides a better fit to the top quartile of wealth holdings than other simple frequency distributions such as the normal or lognormal (see, for example, Atkinson and Harrison 1978a). The value of the Pareto coefficient can be derived from a graph of the logarithm of $N(w)$ against the logarithm of w. It can also be computed from data on the share of wealth owned by the top wealth groups. The estimates reported in this chapter are based on Pareto distributions that give accurate predictions of both the numbers of top wealth holders and their share of total wealth.

3. Although long series of wealth distribution statistics are available for very few other countries, this is true for the U.K. over the 1960, 1970, and 1980 periods. Over a longer timespan, figures assembled for the U.K. by Shorrocks (1987) show that the share of the top 1 percent of individuals fell from 61 percent in 1923 to 23 percent in 1980, while the share of the top 10 percent decreased from 89 percent to 58 percent over the same period. For Sweden, Spant (1987) reports that the share of the top 1 percent of households declined from 50 percent to 21 percent between 1920 and 1975, while the share of the top 10 percent fell from 91 percent to 60 percent.

currently comparable figures are likely to be several percentage points lower than the figures in table 2-2. Second, developed economies have well-established state and private pension arrangements that reduce the need for individuals to accumulate other forms of assets to support consumption during retirement. This tends to increase inequality in observed, marketable wealth. Third, a fast-growing economy such as Korea has a higher proportion of "new wealth" than "old wealth" (acquired by previous generations). As self-made fortunes are passed on, the proportion of inherited wealth will increase, raising the share of the richest groups, because it will include both inherited and self-made wealth. All of these factors would support the view that the Korean distribution of personal wealth as represented by this data source is not an outlier compared with other countries when allowance is made for Korea's stage of development.

Table 2-2. International Comparison of the Distribution of Personal Wealth

Country	Economic unit	Data source	Year	Share of Top			
				1%	*5%*	*10%*	*20%*
Korea	Household	Survey	1988	14[a]	31[a]	43	60
Australia	Household	Survey	1966	9	25	36	54
France	Household	Survey	1975	13	30	50	69
Canada	Household	Survey	1970	20	43	58	74
Sweden	Household	Survey	1975	21	44	60	80
New Zealand	Individual	Estate tax	1966	18	45	60	—
France	Individual	Estate tax	1977	19	47	65	86
Australia	Individual	Estate tax	1971	20	41	57	—
United States	Individual	Estate tax	1969	25	44	53	—
United Kingdom	Individual	Estate tax	1980	23	43	58	—
United Kingdom	Individual	Estate tax	1970	30	54	69	—
United Kingdom	Individual	Estate tax	1960	34	60	72	—

— Not available.
a. Pareto distribution estimates.
Source: Davies (1979), Harrison (1979), Kessler and Masson (1987), Shorrocks (1987), and Spant (1987).

Surveys of Financial Assets

The Bank of Korea (BOK) and the Citizens National Bank (CNB) regularly survey holdings of financial assets, as reported in table 2-3. Using either source, the average financial wealth of households is reported to be between 5 and 6 million won in 1988, a little higher than in the KDI survey (see table 2-1). In addition, BOK reported an average level of debt for 1988 of only 1.18 million won, less than half the corresponding KDI figure (3.24 million won). Thus, using BOK data, the net financial wealth of the average household in the BOK survey is about three times the KDI figure. The BOK surveys also record significantly fewer households that claim to have zero financial assets: less than 10 percent of all households compared with 30 percent of households in the KDI survey.

Table 2-3. The Distribution of Household Financial Assets
(million won)

Range per household	BOK 1986	BOK 1987	BOK 1988	NCB 1988
None	5.5	8.1	6.3	
under 0.3	6.8	4.6	2.5	} 10.1
0.3 - 0.5	4.9	3.3	2.4	
0.5 - 1	11.4	9.1	7.5	9.3
1 - 3	32.3	30.1	30.8	29.5
3 - 5	16.0	16.7	19.1	17.2
5 -10	14.8	17.0	19.6	18.7
Over 10	8.3	11.1	11.8	15.2
Average gross financial wealth	4.25	4.79	5.05	5.90
Average debt	1.92	1.26	1.18	—

— Not available.
Source: Bank of Korea (BOK) and Citizens National Bank (CNB).

In order to usefully compare the financial survey data with distribution of wealth data from the KDI survey, the 1988 data collected by BOK and CNB were transformed into actual distributions.[4] This also allows for a comparison with the decile breakdown of financial wealth prepared by Kang (1990). These comparisons are presented in table 2-4 and they show a more equal distribution of financial assets than the KDI data (table 2-1). The share of the top 10 percent declines from 61 percent to about 46 percent, and the share of the bottom half of the distribution rises from 2 percent to about 11 percent. The average decile shares for gross financial assets reported in table 2-4 are almost identical, however, to KDI figures for real asset holdings. This would support the view that the distribution of financial wealth apparently is not significantly different from the distribution of real assets.

Table 2-4. Estimated Decile Shares of Gross Financial Assets

Decile	BOK 1986	BOK 1987	BOK 1988	CNB 1988	Kang 1988	Average decile share
1	0.2	0.1	0.2	0.4	0.1	0.2
2	0.9	0.9	1.4	1.2	1.4	1.1
3	1.9	2.0	2.4	2.0	2.5	2.2
4	2.8	2.8	3.3	2.9	3.9	3.1
5	3.8	4.1	4.9	4.3	5.3	4.5
6	5.5	6.1	6.7	6.0	7.0	6.3
7	7.9	8.2	8.8	8.1	9.2	8.4
8	10.8	11.4	11.7	10.1	12.0	11.4
9	16.0	16.8	17.0	17.2	17.6	16.9
10	50.2	47.7	43.6	46.8	41.0	45.9
Total	100.0	100.0	100.0	100.0	100.0	100.0

Source: Column 5 from the Ph.D. thesis of Kang (1990). Other figures estimated by Pareto interpolation applied to the data in table 2-3.

4. See footnote 2 for the methodology employed.

Surveys of Housing and Household Goods

Residential housing and household goods seem to be more equally distributed than financial assets or gross personal wealth, as expected. The value of homeownership differed aross income deciles by a factor of less than 3 in 1977, and the value of household goods and occupied housing varied by a factor of about 6 (see table 2-5)—much less variation than for asset distributions. It should be noted, however, that households in table 2-5 are grouped by income rather than by wealth. The principle aim of the National Wealth Survey, which is the source for the figures in table 2-5, is to collect data on the physical assets of businesses, but some data were also collected on the incomes and real assets (excluding land) of households. Surveys were conducted in 1968, 1977, and 1988.

Table 2-5. Residential Housing and Household Goods by Income Decile

Income decile	Share of value of residential housing		Share of household goods
	1977 (owned)	1988 (occupied)	
1	7.1	3.6	3.9
2	7.6	6.9	5.3
3	8.3	6.3	6.6
4	8.5	9.0	7.7
5	8.6	6.4	8.3
6	8.3	9.5	9.3
7	9.3	8.7	10.4
8	11.0	11.7	11.8
9	12.4	14.3	14.3
10	18.9	19.5	22.5
Total	100.0	100.0	100.0

Source: EPB, National Wealth Survey, 1977 and 1988.

Surveys of Landownership

The distribution of landholdings in Korea has received a great deal of attention in recent years because the value of land is high, ownership is concentrated, and land prices have been escalating. There are various estimates of the value of land. The Commission on the Public Concept of Landownership reports the total value of land in 1988 to be 216.2 trillion won (US$300 billion), which can be considered a "low" estimate.[5] The Korea Land Development Corporation values total Korean land at 936.9 trillion won (US$1,325 billion), which can be considered a "high" estimate.[6] For our analysis, following Son (1990), a land value of 557.4 trillion won (US$760 billion) was taken, which can be considered a conservative "middle" estimate.[7] At more than four times GNP in 1988, that is a high ratio by international standards, much higher than the comparable figure for the United States (0.7 times GNP) or the United Kingdom (twice GNP).[8]

Only part of the land is owned by private individuals—about 66.1 percent of Korea's total land *area* in 1988, according to the Commission on the Public Concept of Landownership, which does not report the proportion of total land *value* in private hands.[9] Different kinds of land differ widely in value, and ownership varies with land use, so it is unwise to assume that private ownership of 66.1 percent of land area translates into 66.1 percent of land value. The value of the land depends on whether it is a residential, industrial, forest, agricultural, or used for other purposes (see table 2-6). Thus, for

5. The Commission assumed that the ratio of assessed prices (used to determine tax liability) to market prices is 35 percent and applied this ratio to the 1985 property tax base, adjusted by the 37 percent land price increase during the 1985-88 period.

6. The Corporation sampled 14,038 plots according to category use and administrative district. Each sample was evaluated using market prices and then used to calculate total land value by multiplying the sample average land values by land area in each category (Lee Jin Soon 1990).

7. As suggested by Son (1990), a more realistic figure of 15 percent for the ratio of assessed prices to market prices was applied to the tax base, which was then adjusted for the land price increase reported in Ministry of Construction data during 1985-88, 52 percent.

8. See Lee Jin Soon (1990).

9. It should be noted that a nontrivial part of land classified as owned by private individuals is believed to be owned by corporations.

Table 2-6. Value of Landownership by Private Individuals, 1988
(*trillion won*)

Land use	Total area (km^2)	Area owned by Individuals (percent)	Low value estimate		Middle value estimate		High value estimate	
			Total	Individuals' holdings	Total	Individuals' holdings	Total	Individuals' holdings
Residential	1,854	82.6	125.9	104.0	324.6	268.1	388.4	320.8
Industrial	188	11.2	10.3	1.1	26.6	2.8	47.9	5.4
Forest	65,651	62.5	11.5	7.2	29.6	18.6	127.5	79.7
Agricultural	22,441	91.9	63.9	58.8	164.7	151.6	216.4	199.0
Other uses	9,088	21.2	4.6	1.0	11.9	2.6	156.7	33.2
Total	99,222	66.1	216.2	172.1	557.4	443.7	936.9	638.0

Source: Lee Jin Soon (1990) for high-value estimate; Commission on the Public Concept of Landownership (1989) for low-value estimate; World Bank estimates, for middle-value estimate.

instance, although private individuals own 66 percent of total land area, they hold an estimated 80 percent of total land value. These data must be viewed as providing rough orders of magnitude, because prices of land by category use and administrative district are not fully available. The most startling finding is that the total estimated market value for personal landholdings (444 trillion won) works out to be 42 million won (US$58,000) per household, higher than in many developed countries. There is no doubt that the most valuable tangible assets in Korea today are in the form of land, and this has significant implications for housing, income distribution, and industrial location.

The highly inequitable concentration of landholdings can be seen by looking at table 2-7. The top 5 percent of landowners own 65.2 percent of total land area, the top 10 percent own 76.9 percent, and the top 25 percent own 90.8 percent. This pattern is repeated in each of the large cities, and within each category of land use. The greatest concentration of ownership is in forestland, where the top 10 percent own 93.5 percent of the total area.

Table 2-7. Concentration of Landownership

| Area | Share of landowners | | | Landownings households (percent) |
	top 5 percent	top 10 percent	top 25 percent	
All Korea	65.2	76.9	90.8	n.a.
City				
Seoul	57.7	65.9	77.8	28.1
Pusan	72.3	81.4	89.5	33.1
Daegu	72.6	82.4	92.4	38.3
Inchon	64.2	77.8	88.8	30.1
Kwangju	55.7	69.4	88.4	69.7
Daejon	65.1	76.4	88.2	41.1
Use				
Residential	59.7	65.1		
Industrial	35.1	53.1		
Forest	84.1	93.5		
Paddy field	29.5	47.5		
Barley field	31.9	48.3		
Other	64.8	73.2		

n.a. Not available.
Source: Commission on the Public Concept of Landownership (1989).

Table 2-8. The Degree of Inequality in Landholdings

	Gini coefficient value	
	Landowners	*All households*
Seoul	0.71	0.91
Pusan	0.85	0.95
Daegu	0.87	0.94
Inchon	0.81	0.94
Kwangju	0.81	0.84
All Korea	0.85	n.a.

n.a. Not available.
Source: Commission on the Public Concept of Landownership (1989).

Landownership is even more concentrated when you take into account households that own no land at all—more than half of the population. Only 28 percent of households in Seoul own land, which raises the Gini concentration value from 0.71 for the distribution of land among landowners to 0.91 for the distribution of land among all households (see table 2-8). Comparison with the earlier reported Gini values of 0.58 for gross personal wealth and 0.77 for financial assets indicate the severity of land concentration in Korea. The relative inequality of asset holdings compared with income is seen vividly in figure 2-1, as is the relative concentration among forms of wealth.[10]

To investigate the implications of landownership on the distribution of wealth in more detail, estimates were derived by applying a Pareto fit to the top tail of land distribution, assuming that the shares of land value owned by the top 5 percent and 10 percent of landowners in all of Korea correspond to the shares of land area indicated in table 2-7, and that there were 10.8 million landowners[11] and 25 million adults as of 1988. The results reported in table 2-9 suggest that 10 percent of

10. Distributions of income, gross wealth, and financial assets are taken from KDI Survey (table 2-1) and distribution of land statistics are from *Report of the Commission on the Public Concept of Landownership* (table 2-9).
11. Kwon (1990).

adults own more than 77 percent of total land value in private hands, that 5 percent own 65 percent, and 1 percent own 44 percent. The estimates also suggest that the landholdings of more than 40,000 individuals can be valued at more than 1 billion won in 1988, that more than 2,000 people own land valued at more than 10 billion won, and that more than 90 individuals own land worth at least 100 billion won (US$140 million). Thus, as suggested by figure 2-1, landholdings in Korea are a major source of wealth inequality.

Figure 2-1. Estimated Lorenz Curves: Family Income and Assets

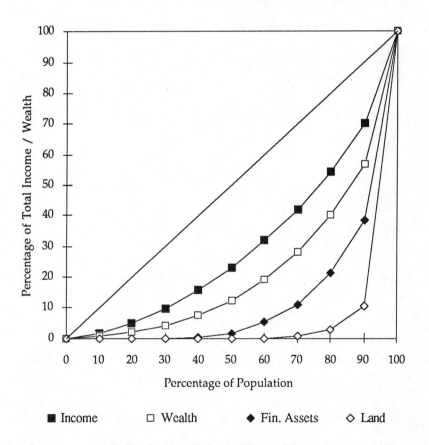

Note: Lorenz curves depict the cumulative holdings of income or wealth by a progressively larger portion of the population. The greater the divergence from the dotted line of perfect quality, the more unequal the distribution.

The distribution of landownership in Korea is a sensitive issue because land values have been escalating for more than a decade. Between 1974 and 1989, for example, land prices rose by a factor of 14, more than three times as fast as real GNP or the consumer price index (see figure 1-2). Over the same period, land prices in Seoul rose by a factor of more than 25. As a result, huge capital gains have accrued to a fraction of the population. Capital gains from landownership have exceeded GNP in many years (see table 2-10). In such circumstances, income distribution figures that exclude capital gains from the sale of land do not accurately reflect the distribution of real income available to households.

Table 2-9. Distribution of Land Value among Individuals

Percentage of population		Percentage share of total land value	Number of landowners
Landowners	All adults		
1	0.4	43.9	
5	2.2	65.2	
10	4.3	76.9	
20	8.6	87.6	
25	10.8	90.8	
30	13.0	92.9	
40	17.3	96.1	
50	21.6	98.0	
100	43.2	100.0	

Estimated holdings

over 1 billion won	40,106
over 10 billion won	2,149
over 100 billion won	93

Source: Commission on the Public Concept of Landownership (1990), and World Bank calculations.

Table 2-10. Capital Gains from Land

Year	Rate of increase in land values (percent)	Capital gain $(10^{12}$ won) (A)	GNP $(10^{12}$ current won) (B)	Ratio A/B
1975	27.0	14.8	10.1	1.5
1980	11.7	24.0	36.7	0.7
1985	7.0	24.4	78.1	0.3
1986	7.3	27.1	90.5	0.3
1987	14.7	58.7	105.6	0.6
1988	27.5	125.9	123.6	1.0
1989	30.5	178.1	137.1	1.3

Source: Lee Jin Soon (1990) and World Bank estimates.

Wealth Statistics Revisited

The problem with sample surveys of wealth holdings is that wealthier households are more likely to refuse to cooperate (a sample selection bias) and that all households may fail to mention, or understate the value of, some of the assets they own (a valuation bias). This latter problem is more severe for wealthier households, which are more prone to undervalue their assets and thus bias the overall results to a larger extent. The magnitude of the problem is difficult to identify and rectify but can be gauged by comparing survey-based estimates of average holdings of different types of assets with other estimates obtained independently. To this end, the personal wealth of households has been subdivided into the main components of real assets (land, buildings, business assets, household goods) and financial assets (cash, savings accounts, bonds, corporate equity, insurance policies, debts), and the value of these components have been estimated for 1988. This allows for the construction of a balance sheet for wealth (see table 2-11) in much the same way the national income accounts construct a balance sheet for income items. (See appendix 2-1 for details of the methodology used.)

Table 2-11. Balance Sheet for Net Personal Wealth, 1988

Asset Category	Low estimate Value (trillion won)	Percent	Middle estimate Value (trillion won)	Percent	High estimate Value (trillion won)	Percent
Real assets	364.8	81.9	636.4	88.7	830.7	91.1
Land	172.1	38.6	443.7	61.9	638.0	70.0
Residential	104.0	23.3	268.1	37.4	320.8	35.2
Nonresidential	68.1	15.3	175.6	24.5	317.2	34.8
Buildings	120.9	27.1	120.9	16.9	120.9	13.3
Residential	83.0	18.6	83.0	11.6	83.0	5.1
Other	37.9	8.5	37.9	5.3	37.9	4.2
Business assets	28.7	6.4	28.7	4.0	28.7	3.1
Household goods	43.1	9.7	43.1	6.0	43.1	4.7
Gross financial assets	138.1	31.0	138.1	19.3	138.1	15.2
Cash	5.4	1.2	5.4	0.8	5.4	0.6
Savings deposits	53.5	12.0	53.5	7.5	53.5	5.9
Bonds	15.7	3.5	15.7	2.2	15.7	1.7
Corporate equity	43.4	9.7	43.4	6.1	43.4	4.8
Insurance policies	20.1	4.5	20.1	2.8	20.1	2.2
Gross personal wealth	502.9	112.9	774.5	108.0	968.8	106.3
Debts	57.4	12.9	57.4	8.0	57.4	6.3
Net personal wealth	445.5	100.0	717.1	100.0	911.4	100.0

Source: World Bank estimates.

Land is clearly the most important component of personal wealth in Korea, and the distribution of land shapes the distribution of personal wealth. But land is also the most difficult item to value. For this reason, three sets of figures are provided — low estimate, middle estimate, and high estimate. Using the low estimate, the total wealth of households in 1988 is an estimated 445 trillion won—39 percent of it attributable to land. Using the middle estimate, the total wealth of households is an estimated 717 trillion won, of which 62 percent is value of land. Using the high estimate, total net personal wealth amounts to 911 trillion won, 70 percent of it attributable to the value of land. The average of household wealth in Korea according to the middle estimate (68 million won, or US$93,000) is very high by international standards, on a par with some developed countries.[12]

A comparison of the balance sheet and survey estimates tends to confirm that wealthy households with large holdings of stocks and bonds are not being properly captured by the survey data (see table 2-12). Nevertheless, the surveys perform reasonably well—certainly as

Table 2-12. Comparison of Survey and Balance Sheet Estimates of Wealth, 1988

	Average household wealth (million won)				
	Balance sheet figure[a]			Survey estimates	
Asset category	Low estimate	Middle estimate	High estimate	KDI[b]	BOK
Real assets	34.7	60.6	79.1	49.0	—
Residential land and buildings	17.8	33.4	38.5	28.8	—
Other real estate	10.1	20.3	33.8	18.1	—
Other real assets	6.8	6.8	6.8	2.0	—
Gross financial assets	13.2	13.2	13.2	4.5	5.1
Cash and savings deposits	5.6	5.6	5.6	—	3.8
Stocks and bonds	5.6	5.6	5.6	—	0.6
Insurance policies	2.0	2.0	2.0	—	0.7
Gross personal wealth	47.9	73.8	92.3	53.5	—
Debts	5.5	5.5	5.5	3.2	1.2
Net personal wealth	42.4	68.3	86.8	50.2	—

— Not available.

a. Computed from Table 2.11, assuming 10.5 million households.

b. Additional figures kindly provided by the Korea Development Institute. (The value of average household wealth differs slightly from table 2-1.)

Source: World Bank estimates.

12. A study by Tachibanaki (1989) for Japan, for 1981, reports average household wealth of about 20 million yen (US$91,000) at 1981 prices.

well as expected on the basis of other countries' experience. The surveys do best on real estate and savings deposits, picking up about 80 percent of the balance sheet value. The KDI (but not the BOK) survey also does well at picking up debt. Business assets and household goods fare less well, and the value of stocks and bonds in the BOK survey is only one-tenth of the balance sheet estimate—which is not unexpected.

There are two practicable ways to adjust for the biases of sample selection and undervaluation of assets involved in sample surveys. The first approach is to take the amount of wealth holdings in the constructed balance sheet (table 2-11) and assume that the distribution of land is the same as in table 2-9 and the distribution of assets other than land is similar to the KDI distribution of gross wealth (table 2-1). The second approach is to adjust gross wealth holdings in the KDI survey to be consistent with figures in the constructed balance sheet with alternative assumptions for the allocation of the undervalued portion of wealth among households. While the preferred approach for the future would be based on balance sheet estimates, this approach may not be suitable for policy analysis because a fair amount of statistical discrepancy can be attached to each component of wealth holdings. (For details of the results of the first approach, see appendix 2-1.) Therefore, although the KDI survey is also subject to statistical error, the second approach has been chosen for our analysis as the baseline estimate.

Thus, to correct for the biases from sample selection and undervaluation of assets, the KDI survey results were adjusted to reflect three different assumptions (see table 2-13). Adjustment A, which raises the average household wealth to the balance sheet estimate, assumes that the difference in the KDI survey is entirely the result of the same degree of undervaluation by all households. This adjustment maintains the relative wealth holdings of all households, so the shares of wealth are identical to those reported in table 2-2. Adjustment B assumes that approximately half of the difference between KDI and balance sheet figures for average wealth is created by underreporting of the very richest households and the remaining half by the same degree of underreporting by all households. Adjustment B raises the top shares of wealth by about 5 percentage points (see table 2-13).

Adjustment C assigns all of the missing wealth to the wealthiest households. This raises the top shares of wealth by a further 5 percentage points. That these different assumptions generate a wide range of values for the top shares of wealth highlights the importance that government should attach to improving the data reporting for wealth statistics.[13]

Table 2-13. Adjusted KDI Figures on Distribution of Wealth

Category	Adjustment A	Adjustment B	Adjustment C
Percentage of wealth owned			
Top 1 percent	14.2	19.2	23.7
Top 5 percent	30.9	36.7	41.4
Top 10 percent	43.1	48.4	52.6
Top 20 percent	60.1	63.9	66.9
Number of holdings			
Over 1 billion won	24,269	35,876	43,057
Over 10 billion won	288	770	1,273
Over 100 billion won	3	17	38

Note: Adjustment A assumes that all households undervalue personal wealth by 22 percent (68.3 million won of middle estimate in table 2-12/55.9 million won in table 2-1 = 1.22). Adjustment B assumes that all households undervalue assets by 10 percent, and that 12 percent of wealth is missing because of the nonresponse of the wealthiest households. Adjustment C assumes that all missing wealth is due to the nonresponse of the wealthiest households. These adjustment are based on Pareto distribution fit.
Source: World Bank estimates.

It may be interesting to compare Korea's household wealth inequality (based on adjustment B) with that of advanced countries,

---

13. The figures for adjustment A suggest that Korea is among the more equal countries reported in table 2-2; with adjustment C the shares of the wealthiest groups are among the highest recorded. For purposes of further analysis, adjustment B is used as the most likely. The complete decile distribution for adjustment B used to generate income flows in chapter 1 is shown in table 2-17 of appendix 2-1.

although the reference years are not directly comparable (see table 2-2). Although the top 10 percent and top 20 percent shares of wealth in Korea are relatively less concentrated, the top 1 percent and top 5 percent shares are relatively more concentrated (see figure 2-2).

Figure 2-2. Household Wealth Inequality

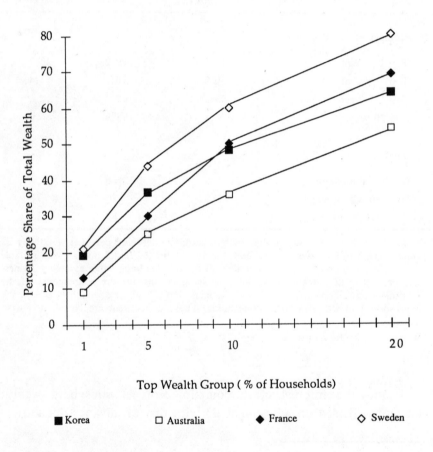

Note: Data are not contemporaneous in time.
Source: Davies (1979), Harrison (1979), Kessler and Masson (1987), Shorrocks (1987), and Spant (1987).

Summary and Conclusions

Findings

Several conclusions emerge from analysis of these statistics on the distribution of wealth in Korea. These are summarized in table 2-14. First, considerable wealth is concentrated in the hands of the top 1 percent of the population—almost exclusively through landownership. This is decidedly at variance with the stated objectives of the Fifth and Sixth Republics and Korea's historical redistribution of land, which formed the basis for its highly participatory growth record. The really large fortunes depend on landownership more than is suggested by landownership's 70 percent share in personal wealth. Focusing, for example, only on individuals worth more than 100 billion won, landowners are 25 times as numerous as corporate stockholders. Available evidence supports what is commonly believed in Korea: that the avenue to great personal wealth is landownership and real estate development rather than investment in manufacturing or other businesses. This conflicts with the economic priorities of the Korean government, as enunciated in the Seventh Five Year Plan documents and other public pronouncements.

Data Needs

Estimates of the distribution of wealth are only as good as the data sources from which they are derived. Korea has a rich collection of potentially useful data that—properly reported and processed—could provide figures as reliable as those for any country in the world. Considerable use has been made of the KDI survey of income and assets in this chapter. But the KDI survey does not seem to fully capture the wealth of the richest households, either because they refuse to respond or because they understate the value of their assets. The revised KDI figures, based on adjustment B or C (see table 2-13), are probably more reliable estimates of the true shares of wealth.

More instruments like the KDI survey are needed, with particular attention to the wealthiest group (perhaps by oversampling). Accurate values should be determined for all kinds of assets. Regular production of a personal sector balance sheet such as table 2-11 would

Table 2-14. Statistics on the Distribution of Wealth in Korea, 1988

Data source	Factor measured	Reference population	Share					Number		
			Top 1%	Top 5%	Top 10%	Top 20%	Over 1 billion won	Over 10 billion won	Over 100 billion won
KDI	Gross wealth	Households	14	30	43	60	—	—	—
KDI	Real assets	Households	—	—	44	61	—	—	—
KDI	Financial assets	Households	—	—	61	78	—	—	—
BOK	Financial assets	Households	—	—	44	61	—	—	93
CPCLO	Land	Landowners	44	65	77	88	40,106	2,149	93
CPCLO	Land	All adults	53	79	90	97	40,106	2,149	93
KDI-adjustment A	Gross wealth	Households	14	31	43	60	24,269	288	3
KDI-adjustment B	Gross wealth	Households	19	37	48	64	35,876	770	17
KDI-adjustment C	Gross wealth	Households	24	41	53	67	43,057	1,273	38
Inheritance tax records	Net wealth	Estates	30	45	54	65	—	—	—
Share registers	Corporate stock	Shareholdings	43	58	66	—	1,461	93	5
Share registers	Corporate stock	Shareowners	41	56	64	—	1,723	—	6

— Not available.

facilitate evaluation of the accuracy of survey results and would provide a basis for correcting the deficiencies of data from sample surveys and other sources.

Inheritance tax returns are currently not terribly useful as a source of information on wealth holdings or wealth transfers. (See appendix 2-2 for a fuller discussion.) Inheritance tax evasion seems to be widespread. It would therefore be useful for the tax authorities to computerize their records and investigate the apparently low size of estates reported.

Policy Implications

That wealth is highly skewed and in all probability becoming more skewed over time poses the policy dilemma of how, if government so chooses, to deal with this phenomenon. Egalitarianism has been a strong force in Korea's development, and conspicuous consumption was actively discouraged, at least during the Third Republic. Government still acts in an ad hoc manner to thwart "excessive wealth" gains, but these measures are largely ineffective. The findings indicate that land and real estate holdings have the most pronounced impact on the distribution of wealth. Land revaluation is clearly the first order of business in accurately assessing the value of asset holdings and providing a proper basis for both property taxes and capital gains taxes. The extent to which income generated by asset holdings (rental income or capital gains) is captured by the Korean tax system requires further examination.

Ownership of financial assets, although a much smaller share of total wealth, is also highly concentrated, and the method of taxation of income derived from those assets is crucial for the distribution of unearned income. Issues of horizontal equity need to be examined amid the widespread perception that wage earners face discriminatory taxation. In assessing the Korean tax system, and its link to the distribution of income, the distribution of wealth is a useful backdrop, although it must be recognized that taxes are not primarily designed to redistribute wealth, and some would argue not even to redistribute income. Nonetheless, the tax system provides government with the most far-reaching set of policy instruments in order to progressively generate tax revenue, while preserving horizontal equity. The extent to which these goals of Korean policy are being met should be reexamined in light of evidence concerning the income and wealth of the richest segment of society.

Policy Lessons

There is a general paucity of official data on wealth holdings in all countries. This problem is often more pronounced in developing countries, particularly those growing rapidly. Wealth survey data has been shown to be rather insensitive to real changes in the value of assets in Korea. Landholdings are shown to be the most skewed asset, followed by financial assets and total wealth. The major lesson for rapidly industrializing economies is not to be complacent about only measuring changes in the distribution of income without intensifying efforts to measure wealth gains.

A major area of concern in a number of rapidly industrializing economies is the market for land. In a number of countries, rigid rules on urban land use, including zoning and cumbersome regulatory procedures, have contributed to skyrocketing land values. This has caused a number of problems. Primary among these is the increasing inability of working people to find affordable housing. In Korea, real incomes, when measured as the ability to purchase housing services, have not risen in the Seoul metropolitan area in the last decade despite massive real income gains. This points to the need to reexamine housing policies, provide housing finance, and, most important, alter both methods of tax administration and access to finance that lead to widespread speculation in land and real estate.

The tax system and the changes needed are described in the following chapter. Suffice it to say, however, that both the design and administration of taxes on real assets need review in countries — such as Korea — that have experienced a doubling of income every decade since 1960. In the Korean context, the generation of wealth cannot be separated from government's official policy of subsidizing the cost of capital and of encouraging the growth of large firms, the jaebols or conglomerates, that dominate Korean industry today. Korea's industrial policy of funneling scarce credit to rapidly growing companies encouraged the formation of large, heavily indebted groups. The risks of this industrial strategy were ultimately borne by government, and the Korean taxpayer, so that those using capital (the entrepreneurial class) benefitted greatly from Korea's industrial development. Recent labor strife points to the fact that wage earners in Korea now feel that the rewards to entrepreneurship are too great compared with the gains accruing to labor.

Korean policymakers and politicians are now experiencing the need to deal straightforwardly with issue of wealth distribution. This is only fitting—the unrealized capital gains accruing to the holders of land and real estate have exceeded GNP in recent years. Government's response has included both useful generalizable elements and classic Korean responses. Greater attention is being given to enforcement of inheritance taxes, often weakly administered in many countries. Land and real estate assessments are being revised to bring greater realism to tax obligations. Loopholes, particularly for the self-employed, are being closed. And the Office of National Tax Administration is being invigorated. These are all useful steps. Some ad hoc measures were also introduced by government to force conglomerates to sell "excessive landholdings" and to force conglomerates to halt speculative land purchases. These are less useful, because they substitute for effective land policy and effective financial policy reform. They do reflect the public's concerns, however, with issues of wealth distribution.

The major lesson arising from an assessment of wealth issues in Korea is that distortions in the accumulation of wealth derive from distortions in the financial system itself. Even if the tax system were reformed to remove biases currently favoring the owners of capital (including the so-called "no name system" of using fictitious names for financial accounts and the generally lax rules on insider trading of securities), it is the underpricing of capital and preferential access to that capital that has both powered Korea's miraculous export drive and phenomenal growth, but it also created pockets of wealth that are now a major policy concern.

Appendix 2-1: Construction of a Balance Sheet for Personal Wealth

The balance sheet estimates of the aggregate value of land owned by individuals are the figures based on low, middle, and high estimates reported in table 2-6. Following is a description of the method for calculating the other figures appearing in the balance sheet on table 2-11.

Real Assets. Estimates of several components of personal sector real assets are provided by the National Wealth Survey for 1988. In the context of real assets, personal sector holdings have been taken to include the assets of households and unincorporated private businesses; personal sector equity in the real assets owned by incorporated businesses are, of course, covered indirectly in corporate stocks value. The National Wealth Survey (volume 1, table 14-2) suggests figures of 41.6 trillion won and 17.5 trillion won, respetively, for the value of buildings owned by households and unincorporated private businesses. The physical assets (other than buildings) and inventories of unincorporated firms are valued at 28.7 trillion won, and household goods at 43.1 trillion won.

These figures allow for depreciation over time. This seems appropriate in the case of business assets and household goods, but less obviously correct for buildings. That household goods are estimated to be worth more than the buildings owned by households seems especially odd. the National Wealth Survey (volume 1, table 14-1) provides alternative figures for the gross (cost price) value of buildings that, at roughly double the net values, are more in line with expectations. These figures have therefore been used, giving figures of 83.0 trillion won and 37.9 trillion won for the value of buildings owned by households and unincorporated private business, respectively.

Financial Assets. Values for most of the financial components are derived from the flow of funds data for the end of 1988 (Bank of Korea, 1990, page 331). The figures given for cash and savings deposits are 5.4 and 53.5 trillion won, respectively. The value of bonds ("short-term securities" plus "long-term securities") is reported as 15.7 trillion won, and personal sector debt (including government loans and trade credit) as 51.6 trillion won. The flow of funds accounts also record a "miscellaneous" net liability of 5.8 trillion won, yielding total debt of 57.4 million won.

Personal sector holdings of corporate equity are more difficult to estimate. The flow of funds data give figures of 10.3 trillion won for "stocks" and 5.2 trillion won for "equities other than stocks." But corporate stock is valued at the issue price rather than the market price. According to the flow of funds data, individuals own 48.6 percent of the total value of corporate stock, with a reported market value in 1988 of 78.7 trillion won (Bank of Korea 1990, page 329, footnote). A reasonable estimate of the personal sector holdings of stocks is therefore 78.7 x 48.6 percent = 38.2 trillion won, to which the "equities other than stocks" figure may be added to yield a personal sector corporate equity of 43.4 trillion won.

This figure for personal sector holdings of corporate stock may be thought to be an overestimate, because 1988 was the year in which the state-owned Pohang Iron & Steel Company (POSCO) was sold to the public. The ratio of market price to issue price for POSCO shares is lower than the average for all listed stocks, so it would not be appropriate to scale up the nominal value of private sector stock in the same proportion as other stock if POSCO shares were disproportionately held by individuals. A large proportion of POSCO shares, however, are held by financial institutions and the Ministry of Finance. Furthermore, a comparison of the flow of funds figures for 1987 and 1988 reveals that the personal sector holdings of corporate stock (at issue price) fell from 55.5 percent to 48.6 percent between 1987 and 1988. So there is no reason to suppose that the personal sector held less than 48.6 percent of the market value of corporate stock in 1988: indeed the ratio may have exceeded this figure.

The last financial asset to be included in the personal sector balance sheet is the value of holdings in life insurance and pension funds, given as 20.1 trillion won in the flow of funds accounts. Combining all these items suggests a figure of 80.7 trillion won for the net financial assets of the personal sector. This compares with the figure of 52.8 trillion won given in the flow of funds accounts, the difference represented by the revaluation of corporate stock from issue price to market price.

Wealth Distribution Based on the Personal Balance Sheet

There are many wealthy individuals in Korea—more than 30,000 people worth more than 1 billion won each (US$1.4 million). The best way to estimate what share of total wealth the richest households own may be to separate land from other forms of household assets. Assuming that the distribution of land among households is the same as the distribution of land among landowners, and that assets other than land are distributed similarly to the KDI distribution of gross wealth, the richest 1 percent of households own about 33 percent of all wealth (see table 2-15), the top 5 percent own 52 percent of the wealth, the top 10 percent own 64 percent, and the top 20 percent own 77 percent.

In other words, the top 20 percent of households own 77 percent of the wealth, and the bottom 80 percent of households own 23 percent of the wealth. A 64 percent share for the top 10 percent of households is not exceptionally high by the standards of developed countries, but a 33 percent share for the top 1 percent is much higher than for most of the countries listed in table 2-2.

It is difficult to say whether the distribution of wealth in Korea has become more or less unequal over time for lack of time series data. It depends on how fast land values have increased in relation to the value of other assets. Between 1980 and 1987, for example, land prices doubled, so the value of land owned by the top 10 percent of the population increased, but GNP rose even faster, so the value of other assets is likely to have increased faster than the value of land. As a result, the share of total wealth owned by the top 10 percent of households is estimated to have fallen slightly, from 66 percent to 63 percent. The rapid escalation of land prices that began in 1987 reversed this trend, moving the share of the top 10 percent back up to 65 percent, which it had been in 1981 (see table 2-16). Finally, land is so important a factor in wealth that the single best way to make figures on the distribution of wealth more reliable would be to supplement available data on landownership by area with data on landownership by value.

Table 2-15. Proportionate Ownership of Korea's Wealth

Group	Land Value (trillion won)	Land Share (percent)	Other assets Value (trillion won)	Other assets Share (percent)	Total wealth Value (trillion won)	Total wealth Share (percent)
Top 1 percent	195	44	38	14	233	33
Top 5 percent	289	65	82	30	371	52
Top 10 percent	341	77	118	43	459	64
Top 20 percent	390	88	164	60	554	77
Bottom 80 percent	54	12	109	40	163	23
All households	444	100	273	100	717	100

Note: Figures are by household in 1988.
Source: Staff estimates and compilations.

The distribution of real assets is broadly similar to that of financial assets. (This was noted in connection with the KDI results for real assets and the bank surveys of financial assets, and is evident when comparing the distribution of land among landowners and the distribution of listed corporate stock among shareowners.) Distributions among individuals (landowners and shareowners) are markedly more concentrated than other distributions shown on table 2-14. This indicates a degree of substitutability between real and financial assets: the richest landowners are not always the richest shareowners as well. It also reflects the tendency (in all countries) for wealth to be more unequal among individuals than among households (see table 2-2).

Table 2-16. Trends in Inequality of Wealth in Korea, 1980-1989
(trillion won)

Year	Top 10 percent			All households			Share of top 10 percent
	Land	Other	Total	Land	Other	Total	
1980	134	35	169	174	81	255	66
1981	144	43	187	187	100	287	65
1982	152	50	202	197	115	312	65
1983	179	59	238	234	136	370	64
1984	203	67	270	264	155	419	64
1985	218	75	293	283	173	456	64
1986	234	86	320	303	200	503	64
1987	268	101	369	348	233	581	63
1988	341	118	459	444	273	717	64
1989	451	132	583	585	305	890	65

Note: Estimates are based on table 2-15. The value of nonland assets is assumed to have risen in line with GNP.

Table 2-17. Wealth Shares Calculated from KDI Data Using Adjustment B

Decile	Share
1	0.5
2	1.2
3	2.0
4	3.1
5	4.4
6	6.0
7	8.1
8	10.8
9	15.5
10	48.4
Aggregate value (trillion won)	717.7

Note: Figures are calculated for table 2-13. Adjustment B assumes all households undervalue assets by 10 percent and that a similar amount of the "missing wealth" is the result of nonreporting by the richest households.

Appendix 2-2: Further Potential Sources of Data

Inheritance tax returns and registers of shareholdings appear never to have been used before for as sources of data about the distribution of wealth in Korea. Their analysis here is necessarily limited in scope, but provides additional information on the topic of wealth as well as some guidance for future research efforts.

Inheritance and Gift Tax Records. A common method of estimating wealth holdings in other countries is to treat the estates of those who die as representative of the holdings of the living. First, the number and value of estates is separated by age and gender, then each figure is scaled up proportionate to the full population, using the inverse of the corresponding mortality rate. Korea's inheritance tax is a tax on total estates (rather than inheritances received), so inheritance tax data could be a good basis for estimating wealth—except that considerable inheritance tax evasion mars the data.

The way in which inheritance data is reported in Korea is not ideal for the purpose of estimating the distribution of wealth. To begin with, the grouping of individuals by taxable estate (see table 2-18) does not correspond to the grouping of individuals by gross estate (the average gross value in column 3 of table 2-18 does not always increase in proportion to the size of the net estate). In addition, ONTA was unable to supply figures by age and gender, so age and sex mortality multipliers cannot be applied. Without those details, attention was focused on the distribution of wealth among people who died in 1988—in other words, the distribution of estate size, including estates not recorded in inheritance tax data. The number of deaths of adults age twenty or over recorded in 1988 was 177,480. So the 1,414 estates valued for inheritance tax purposes represent less than 1 percent of the population under consideration. If mortality was random, the distribution of estate size could be used to estimate the distribution of wealth among the living. But mortality and wealth both vary greatly with age, so estates are not a random sample of general holdings of wealth. It is difficult to determine the relationship between the distribution of estate size and the distribution of personal wealth with any precision.

Table 2-18. The Number and Value of Estates, 1988

Taxable estate [a] (million won)	Number of estates	Gross value (billion won)	Average gross value (million won)
under 1	189	4.6	24
1-3	83	4.0	48
3-5	46	3.3	72
5-7	65	4.4	67
7-10	68	6.3	93
10-13	73	6.2	85
13-19	88	7.9	90
19-25	91	9.7	106
25-35	107	11.4	107
35-50	93	13.8	148
50-70	122	18.3	150
70-100	95	17.4	184
100-300	193	51.5	267
300-500	37	19.0	514
500+	64	83.5	1305
Total	1,414	261.4	185

a. Net of allowances and exemptions.
Source: ONTA (1989, page 80).

Figures on the portfolio composition of estates are broadly similar to those derived from the balance sheet of personal wealth. The asset shares calculated for estates typically lie between the balance sheet figures based on low estimate and middle estimate for land, with some exceptions (see table 2-19). The almost total neglect of household goods in the valuation of estates gives a low asset share for the "other real assets" component. In addition, the share of corporate stock in estates is higher than the balance sheet figure, and the share of cash, savings deposits, and bonds is lower. This probably reflects the slightly different composition of the wealth holdings of the richer groups captured in the estate data.

Table 2-19. Value of Estates by Category of Asset, 1988

Asset category	Estate value (billion won)	Percent of gross estate	Percent of gross wealth [a]		
			Low estimate	Middle estimate	High estimate
Real assets	187.3	75.6	72.5	82.1	85.7
Land	136.9	55.3	34.2	57.3	65.9
Residential	83.3	33.7	20.7	34.6	33.1
Nonresidential	53.6	21.6	13.5	22.7	32.7
Buildings	46.4	18.7	24.0	15.6	12.5
Other real assets	4.0	1.6	14.3	9.3	7.4
Gross financial assets	60.3	24.4	27.5	17.9	14.3
Cash	0.6	0.2	1.1	0.7	0.6
Savings deposits	7.7	3.1	10.6	6.9	5.5
Bonds	0.1	0.1	3.1	2.0	1.6
Corporate stock	25.8	10.4	8.6	5.6	4.5
Insurance policies	3.7	1.5	4.0	2.6	2.0
Other financial assets	22.5	9.1	—	—	—
Gross estate[b]	247.6	100.0	100.0	100.0	100.0

— Not available.

a. Based on the balance sheet figures in table 2-11.

b. Excluding gifts.

Source: ONTA (1989, pp. 82-83).

More difficult to reconcile is the difference between the average level of estates and the average level of balance sheet wealth. The raw figures suggest a value of only 1.5 million won (= 261.4/177.5) for the average gross wealth of individuals, a fraction of the balance sheet figure of about 35 million won (using the middle estimate for land). But this takes no account of the wealth of the 99 percent of estates that are not recorded in the inheritance tax tables. These "missing persons" in the estate statistics presumably have net estates below the minimum taxable limit (1 million won). But without tax allowances, the gross estate size could be much larger. Applying a Pareto distribution and the rules for inheritance tax allowances, we calculate that the total value of the missing estates is about 1 trillion won, giving a figure of 1,261 billion won for the total value of estates in 1988, or an average of 7.1 million won for each individual. But this explains only part of the difference between the average size of estates and average balance sheet wealth; a large gap remains.

Part of the discrepancy, we suspect, is because estate wealth is grossly underreported, and inheritance taxes are evaded on a grand scale. Estate valuations of such assets as household goods tend to be low—and a significant amount of cash and savings are probably not reported in estates. Another possibility is that the distribution of estates is not representative of the wealth of the living. The average size of an estate should be greater than the average holding of wealth, because older people are typically wealthier and have higher mortality rates (see Shorrocks 1975 and Greenwood 1987). But richer individuals, particularly those in poor health, have a strong incentive to pass their wealth on to other family members, which may reverse the presumption in favor of larger average estates. Investigating these possibilities requires more information on the distribution of estates by age and gender, and details of the asset composition of estates at different levels of wealth, neither of which ONTA can supply.

If the total value of estates is an estimated 1,261 billion won, the share of the top 1,414 estates (.8 percent of the total number) is at least 20.7 percent (= 261/1261). This suggests that the share of the top 1 percent of estates is at least 23 percent—29.6 percent, if you estimate the value of the missing estates. Following the same principle, the share of the top 5 percent would be 45.3 percent; of the top 10 percent, 54.4 percent; and of the top 20 percent, 65.3 percent. These figures are similar to the numbers under adjustment C of the KDI data (table 2-13)—but they refer to the distribution of individual estates, rather than to household wealth, and the estimated average estate size remains well below the average balance sheet figure.

Registers of Shareholdings. The wealthiest individuals are typically those who have a substantial stake in a public company or own a valuable piece of real estate, which is often revealed by a search of public documents. This is the method *Fortune* magazine uses to construct its annual list of the wealthiest people in the United States and elsewhere. Identifying and valuing the assets of specific individuals is a time-consuming task, made more difficult in Korea by the widespread use of false names in registration documents. It is not a practical method of determining even the share of the wealthiest 1 percent, because this would involve dealing with at least 250,000 individuals. But it does provide a valuable source of information on the wealthiest 1 percent that is not otherwise available.

A detailed search of public records was not possible, but calculations were done using the largest holdings of listed corporate stock in 1988, data reported in Daewoo Securities, "Investment Survey of 160 Companies in the Korean Stock Market" (1989). This publication provides information on 160 major corporations, including the total number of shares, the range of share prices, and the names of major shareholders and their proportionate stake. The market value of each company was taken to be the highest share price in 1988 multiplied by the number of shares; the value of each personal shareholding was then calculated from the percentage of shares held.

The Daewoo Securities booklet lists about three major shareholders in each corporation. It records only 154 personal shareholdings, only 5 of which refer to shareholdings in the top 20 corporations. This is a severe limitation. A 1 percent stake in any one of the 20 largest companies in 1988 was worth about 10 billion won, enough to warrant a place in the largest 100 shareholdings in Korea. But many of these are missing, because the Daewoo publication seldom reports shareholdings under 5 percent. Clearly a more thorough search of share registration data would have revealed more shareholdings over 10 billion won, and many more over 1 billion won.

Roughly 63 percent of the 8.541 million shareholdings in 1988 were owned by individuals (Daewoo Securities 1990, pp. 28 and 31), giving 5.381 million personal shareholdings (see table 2-20). The total market value of listed corporate stock at the end of 1988 was 64.5 trillion won; 48.6 percent of this was in the hands of individuals (Daewoo Securities 1990, page 28; Bank of Korea 1990, page 331). Thus, personally owned listed stock was worth an estimated 31.4 trillion won, or an average 5.8 million won per shareholding. With this information, and the 154 identified shareholdings, table 2-20 was created. The results suggest that the 100 largest shareholdings together comprise more that 10 percent of the total value of listed corporate stock in private hands, and a mere 13 shareholdings represent more than 5 percent of the total value.

More conventional distributional statistics for listed stock were calculated by applying a Pareto distribution to this data. The maximum potential shareholding was assumed to be 500 billion won. Parameters of the distribution were chosen to fit the aggregate stock value of both the top group of shareholders and the whole population. The result was a minimum shareholding of an estimated 1 million won (roughly 50 average-price shares).[1] The Pareto fit accurately predicts the identified number of shareholdings over 50 billion won and 100 billion won (see table 2-21). The divergence between the predicted number of shareholdings and the number of identified shareholdings (table 2-20) increases as we move down the distribution. The Pareto estimates suggest that 78 percent (= 73/93) of the shareholdings over 10 billion won and 53 percent of those above 5 billion won were identified, but relatively few of those valued under 5 billion won. This is very much in line with expectations. As for the total value of shareholdings, the Pareto predictions tend to be higher than the corresponding figures in table 2-20. But they include shareholdings that have not been individually identified—for example, an additional 20 holdings of 10 to 50 billion won, whose aggregate value must be at least 200 billion won, and another 80 holdings of 5 to 10 billion won, with a minimum total value of 400 billion won. Adding this "missing wealth" to the identified value of shareholdings over 5 billion won raises the aggregate value from 3.3 trillion won to 3.9 trillion won, exactly the same as the Pareto estimate.

About 1,450 shareholdings were valued at more than 1 billion won at the end of 1988 (see table 2-21). Only 1 percent of the 5.381 million personal shareholdings were valued at more than 48.7 million won, and only 10 percent exceeded 7.1 million won. The top 1 percent of shareholdings together comprised 42.9 percent of the total value of listed corporate stock in private hands, the top 5 percent comprised 58.3 percent of total stock value, and the top 10 percent comprised 66.2 percent.

---

1. The average share price in December 1988 was 25,700 won.

Table 2-20. Identified Major Shareholdings, 1988

Range of value (billion won)	Number of identified share-holdings	Cumulative number of share-holdings	Value of identified share-holdings (billion won)	Cumulative value of shareholdings (billion won)	Percent of share-holdings
1 - 5	36	149	106	3,454	11.0
5 - 10	40	113	292	3,348	10.7
10 - 50	60	73	1,410	3,056	9.7
50 - 100	8	13	653	1,646	5.2
100+	5	5	993	993	3.2
All shareholders	5,381,000	5,381,000	31,368	31,368	100.0

Source: Daewoo Securities.

The distribution of shareholdings is not, of course, the same thing as the distribution of corporate stock among shareowners, because a single shareowner may own stock in several different companies. To convert from shareholdings to shareowners requires adding these separate holdings together. This is difficult to do, because the data source covers only the major stakes in the larger corporations. But a number of individuals appear more than once in the 154 identified shareholdings, and the values of their holdings have been combined to obtain data on share ownership. The top 50 shareowners in Korea held 2,932 billion won of shares or, 9.3 percent of the total value of listed corporate stock in private hands.

To calculate the share of corporate stock owned by the top groups of shareholders, a Pareto distribution was applied to data on total personal corporate stock and on the holdings of the richest group. To circumvent the problem that the total number of shareowners is unknown (although it clearly cannot be greater than the number of shareholdings), alternative estimates were calculated for populations of 1, 2, and 3 million shareholders. As the total number of shareowners shrinks, the number of individuals in the top p percent of shareowners

Table 2-21. Estimated Distribution of Shareholdings

Minimum value (million won)	Number of shareholdings	Percent	Value of shareholdings (billion won)	Percent
1.0	5,381,000	100.0	31,368	100.0
7.1	538,100	10.0	20,772	66.2
12.6	269,050	5.0	18,281	58.3
48.7	53,810	1.0	13,469	42.9
100	22,785	0.4	11,368	36.2
1,000	1,461		6,314	20.1
5,000	213		3,902	12.4
10,000	93		3,073	9.8
50,000	13		1,525	4.9
100,000	5		993	3.2

Source: Staff estimates.

decreases, and their average number of shareholdings and hence the average value of their stock increases. These two effects work in opposite directions, so the net impact is impossible to predict, but our calculations suggest that the top shares of wealth fall as the number of shareowners decreases (see table 2-22). The effect is small, however, so the distribution of corporate stock among shareowners is little different from the distribution of shareholdings shown in table 2-21. Grouping shareholding figures into shareownership figures does raise the predicted number of won billionaires—from 1,461, based on shareholdings, to about 1,750, based on shareownership—and raises the total holdings of this group of individuals to about 24 percent of listed corporate stock in private hands.

Table 2-22. The Distribution of Listed Corporate Stock

	Percentage of Corporate Stock Owned			
	Shareowners			
Item	*1 million*	*2 million*	*3 million*	*Shareholdings*
Top 1 percent	38	41	42	43
Top 5 percent	53	56	58	58
Top 10 percent	62	64	66	66
Holdings over *1 billion won*				
Number	1,941	1,723	1,621	1,461
Share (percent)	26	24	23	20
Population (million)	1	2	3	5.4

Source: Staff estimates.

3

POLICY ISSUES IN THE KOREAN TAXATION SYSTEM

Overview: Characteristics of Taxation in Korea

The Korean tax system includes both national and local taxes. National taxes are divided into internal taxes, customs duties, and the education tax. The temporary defense tax was repealed effective January 1, 1991, and the temporary education tax became permanent in 1992. The tax system currently functioning in Korea is depicted in chart 3-1. The system has been shaped by two major tax reform measures: the adoption of a global personal income tax in 1975 and the introduction of a value added tax (VAT) in 1977. The former replaced a largely schedular personal income tax system that had been levied separately on each category of income, with a global tax at progressive rates on combined income. The latter streamlined a complicated system of excise and turnover taxes with a single rate VAT.

The ratio of total tax revenue to GNP (the tax burden) in Korea has increased to 19.4 percent in 1990 from an average of about 14 percent in the early 1970s (see table 3-1). Korea's tax burden ratio is only slightly higher than the ratios of developing countries in Asia and is much lower than those of the most developed countries (see table 3-2).[1]

One important characteristic of the tax structure in Korea is its heavy reliance on indirect taxes. As shown in table 3-3, slightly more than half of total tax revenue is derived from indirect taxes in 1989.[2]

---

1. According to a recent study, Korea's actual tax burden ratio is 4 to 6 percentage points lower than the expected ratio, based on regressions of a sample of thirty-three countries. See Shim and Nam (1988).

2. A debate exists over the exact categorization of direct versus indirect taxes. Here we select a standard categorization used in Ministry of Finance (1990a).

Chart 3-1. Tax System in Korea

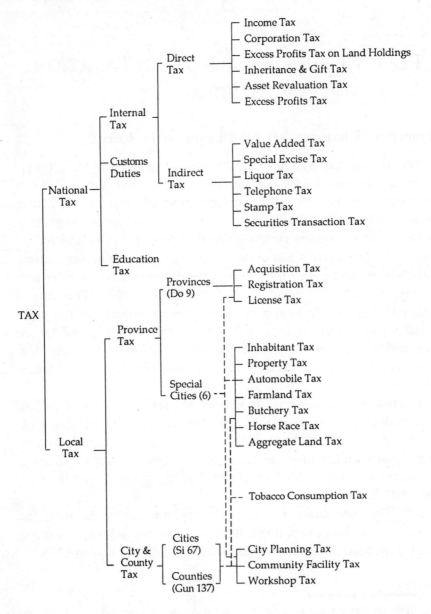

Source: Ministry of Finance (1990b).

Table 3-1. Tax Burden in Korea

Period	Total tax revenue/GNP (percentage)
1971-75 average	13.9
1976-80 average	17.5
1981-85 average	18.2
1986	17.3
1987	17.5
1988	17.9
1989	18.5
1990	19.4

Source: Bank of Korea (1990) and Ministry of Finance (1990b).

Table 3-2. International Comparison of Tax Structure in 1988

Country	Tax burden (percent)	Per capita GNP (US$) [b]	Indirect tax/ total tax [c]	Indirect tax/ total tax [d]
Korea	16.3	3,600	56.8	48.8
Developing countries				
Thailand	15.8	1,000	75.3	67.1
Malaysia	16.7	1,940	50.3	34.0
Philippines[a]	12.1	630	72.4	61.3
Indonesia	15.4	440	33.8	29.3
India[a]	11.7	340	81.4	70.6
Developed countries				
Japan[a]	21.7	21,020	10.9	10.2
United States	18.2	19,840	5.8	4.0
Canada	17.8	16,960	25.4	22.1
United Kingdom[a]	32.7	12,810	34.3	34.2
France	37.9	16,090	31.9	31.8
Federal Republic of Germany	27.3	18,480	23.7	23.7

a. 1987.
b. Based on World Bank Atlas method.
c. Including customs duties.
d. Excluding customs duties.
Source: IMF, *Government Finance Statistical Yearbook*, 1990 and *International Financial Statistics*, 1990; World Bank, *World Development Report*, 1990.

The VAT, in particular, has been a major source of revenue, generating approximately 20 percent of total tax revenue. Data show that Korea's reliance on indirect taxes has been fairly constant over time and that indirect taxes are a more balanced source of revenue in Korea than other Asian countries, such as Thailand and the Philippines. Korea's heavy reliance on indirect taxes is not exceptional compared with other economies with value added tax systems such as France (59.8 percent in 1987) and Taiwan, China (58.7 percent in 1988).[3] Recently, its reliance on indirect taxes has been declining because, in part, of the strengthening of taxation on properties and capital gains.

Table 3-3. Direct and Indirect Tax Ratios

Year	Direct taxes as percent of total	Indirect taxes as percent of total
1970	43.5	56.5
1975	39.5	60.5
1980	36.9	63.1
1985	39.3	60.7
1986	38.9	61.1
1987	41.1	58.9
1988	44.9	55.1
1989	49.8	50.2

Source: Ministry of Finance (1990a).

As shown in table 3-4, the national government collects almost 90 percent of total tax revenue. The major revenue sources for the central government are consumption and income taxes, while the local governments rely on property-related taxes. The distinction between central and local government has little meaning in Korea because local governments have neither the means to introduce new taxes nor the power to change tax rates in response to the needs of local residents.

---

3. Ministry of Finance (1990a).

Table 3-4. The Tax Structure in Korea
(percent)

Category	1980	1985	1989 (budget)
National taxes			
Domestic taxes			
Personal income	10.1	11.1	12.4
Corporation	7.4	8.4	12.3
Inheritance and gift	0.1	0.3	0.5
Assets revaluation	0.3	0.1	0.2
Excess profit	0.0	0.0	0.0
Value added	22.6	21.7	21.1
Special excise	8.9	7.3	5.1
Liquor	4.6	3.8	3.8
Telephone	0.8	1.2	1.1
Stamp	0.5	0.6	0.6
Securities transaction	0.0	0.1	1.1
Customs duties	11.8	11.7	9.6
Surcharges			
Defense tax	13.2	12.7	13.0
Education tax	n.a.	2.4	1.7
Monopoly profits	7.8	6.2	n.a.
Other	1.0	0.9	1.0
Subtotal	89.1	88.5	83.5
Local Taxes			
Ordinary taxes			
Acquisition	2.5	2.7	2.5
Registration	1.9	2.7	3.1
License	0.3	0.2	0.2
Inhabitant	1.8	1.5	1.7
Property	1.8	1.8	1.6
Excess landholding	n.a.	n.a.	0.1
Farmland income	1.0	0.1	0.0
Butchery	0.1	0.1	0.1
Horse race	0.0	0.1	0.1
Tobacco	n.a.	0.6	5.6
Earmarked Taxes			
City planning	0.8	0.9	0.7
Fire service facilities	0.2	0.3	0.3
Workshop	0.5	0.5	0.5
Subtotal	10.9	11.5	16.5
Total	100.0	100.0	100.0

n.a. Not applicable.
Source: Kwack and Lee (1990).

Among the direct taxes that now generate 42 percent of total tax revenue, the role of the personal income tax is relatively insignificant in Korea. Only 13 percent of total tax revenue is collected from individual income taxes. As of 1989, only about 2 percent of GNP was collected as personal income tax, while in most developed countries the level is around 10 percent (Kwack and Lee 1990). The central government's taxes on wealth are also insignificant in terms of their revenue yield. Revenue collected from these taxes accounts for less than 1 percent of the central government's total tax revenue.

Major Taxes in Korea

Personal Income Tax

In principle, Korea has chosen to adopt a global taxation approach to personal income tax. Thus, global personal income includes interest income, dividend income, real estate rental income, business income, and wages and salaries. Global income is taxed according to a highly progressive rate scheme, with the marginal tax rates ranging from 5 to 50 percent for five income brackets. Taking the standard deductions to income, taxation of taxable income begins at approximately 5 percent for the 7th decile and reaches 27 to 50 percent for the top decile. Roughly two-thirds of global income tax is withheld at the source; 70 percent of this is attributable to wages and salaries, and a further 25 percent to the flat rate tax on interest and dividends. Small businesses and those with real estate income account for the bulk of global income tax not withheld at source. Despite the very high and progressive tax rates, personal income tax contributes only 13 percent of government's total tax take, which is very low compared with high-income countries, and surprisingly also below the average for middle- and low-income countries (see table 3-5).

The relative unimportance of the personal income tax is the result of several factors. First, even though the marginal tax rate is very high and progressive, the exemption level is also very high, and only about 40 percent of income earners pay income tax. Second, most interest income and more than half of dividend income is taxed separately, at a low flat rate of 20 percent. Third, capital gains from financial asset transactions are completely untaxed and those from real estate

Table 3-5. Tax Structure by Economic Classification

Tax category	Korea Central + local government			Central Governments				
	1980	1985	1989 budget	Korea 1985	Low-income countries[a] 1985	Middle-income countries[b] 1985	High-income countries[c] 1985	
Taxes on income and profit	25.0	26.7	32.4	29	25	32	35	
Company, corporate, or enterprise	(11.1)	(11.8)	(16.1)	(13)	(9)	(10)	(27)	
Individual	(12.4)	(13.5)	(14.8)	(15)	(15)	(17)	(27)	
Social security contributions	1.1	1.5	4.7	2	1	11	31	
Taxes on property	7.6	8.8	9.7	1	1	2	2	
Inheritance and gift taxes	(0.2)	(0.4)	(0.6)					
Taxes on goods and services	48.1	45.4	38.8	49	32	30	29	
Value added tax	(22.1)	(21.1)	(19.9)					
Taxes on international trade and transactions	15.2	14.2	12.0	16	38	19	2	
Other taxes	3.0	3.5	2.5	3	3	6	1	
Total	100.0	100.0	100.0	100	100	100	100	

a. Unweighted average of seventeen countries (per capita income ranges from US$120 to US$420 in 1986).
b. Unweighted average of thirty-three countries (per capita income ranges from US$460 to US$7,410 in 1986).
c. Unweighted average of seventeen countries (per capita income ranges from US$7,460 to US$17,680 in 1986).
Source: Bank of Korea (1990) and World Bank, *World Development Report*, 1988.

transactions are believed to be seriously undertaxed. Fourth, the general level of income tax compliance, although high for a developing country, could still be raised.

The separate taxation of almost all interest income and about 60 percent of dividend income at only 20 percent in contrast to the very high and progressive rates used in taxing wages and salaries raises a question of equity.[4] That holders of bonds and securities are not forced to use their own names on these instruments exacerbates the problem. Although reportedly 98 percent of financial assets are held under real names rather than fictitious names, a substantial portion of financial assets under supposedly real names are actually under the borrowed names of relatives or friends. (The Korean government postponed indefinitely the introduction of the "real name" system of financial asset transactions in 1990, reminiscent of its actions in 1982.)[5] While the government applies a 60 percent tax rate on interest and dividend income under purely fictitious names, which account for only 2 percent of total financial transactions, this has a negligible effect in terms of distributional equity.

The present level of personal exemptions and deductions seems rather high in relation to Korean income levels and wage rates. In 1989 it was equal to about 1.4 times per capita GNP and about 80 percent of the average earnings of mining and manufacturing workers. Because of the high threshold at which tax becomes payable in relation to average income, only 40 percent of wage and salary earners are liable for any personal income tax; the remaining 60 percent pay none whatsoever. This exemption level is high by international standards (see table 3-6) and effective January 1, 1990 this exemption level was raised further. This is one of the major reasons for the relatively low yield from the global income tax.

---

4. Among the dividends, only presumptive dividends, dividends from major shareholders of listed corporations, and dividends from nonlisted corporations are subject to global taxation.

5. The "real name" system is further discussed in the section entitled "Some Issues in Korean Taxation".

Table 3-6. Exemption Level of Personal Income Tax
(1987)

Economy	Exemption Level/Average Household Income[a] (percent)
Korea	43.5
France	43.0
Japan	32.5
Taiwan, China	26.9
United States	21.9
West Germany	19.7
United Kingdom	19.0
Singapore	8.6

a. Based on a four-member family.
Source: Ministry of Finance (1990a).

A second reason for the low yield of global income tax is the generous treatment of small businesses, which include self-employed professionals such as doctors and lawyers. There have been widespread complaints that employees are heavily taxed in relation to self-employed professionals, and this criticism, together with an excess of tax receipts over budget forecasts, has prompted the government to provide a tax rebate to wage and salary earners in 1989 and 1990.[6] The yield of personal income tax is limited by the 20 percent flat rate tax on interest and dividends and by the capital gains exemptions on financial assets. The net result is that personal income derived from different sources is taxed differentially and inequitably; for example, for monthly wage income of 5 million won, interest income of 5 million won, and capital gains from financial assets of 5 million won, the

---

6. Although further steps are needed, the principle of more equitable tax treatment of self-employed professionals compared with taxation on salary and wage earners was introduced in the 1990 tax reforms.

respective marginal tax rates would be 50 percent, 20 percent, and zero.[7]

Corporation Tax

Corporation tax rates vary depending on the size of income and the type of corporation. For private corporations, a 20 percent tax rate is applied to income of up to 100 million won (US$140,000) and a tax rate of 34 percent for income exceeding 100 million won. Nonprofit corporations are taxed at 20 percent up to 80 million won and at 27 percent thereafter. For public corporations, a 17 percent tax rate is applied to income of up to 300 million won and a 25 percent tax rate thereafter except for Associations of Agriculture, Fisheries, and Livestock, which are taxed at a 10 percent flat rate. For unlisted large-scale corporations that have accumulated and retained 40 percent or more of distributable income, an additional 25 percent tax is levied on the accumulated earnings.

The share of corporate tax revenue in total tax revenue in Korea is fairly low compared with the shares in high-income countries (see table 3-5). This is partly because of complicated tax incentive schemes provided mainly through the Tax Exemption and Reduction Control Law.[8] Although some complicated tax incentive schemes were streamlined considerably by the tax reforms of 1982, incentive measures such as accelerated depreciation, investment tax credits, and tax-free reserves are still liberally used in promoting R&D investment, investment in small and medium industries, and relocation of industries away from large metropolitan areas. The amount of corporate tax lost through the Tax Exemption and Reduction Control Law amounts to 1,478 billion won (US$2 billion), or about 40 percent of actually collected corporate tax revenue in 1989.

Capital Gains Tax on Real Estate

The capital gains tax on real estate has been designed essentially to curb speculation on real estate. In order to discourage the frequent

---

7. Although a 2 percent securities transactions tax is currently levied on sales of securities, this is not a tax on capital gains and its contribution to total tax revenue is trivial.

8. The provisions of the law are temporary and are due to expire after 1991.

turnover of real estate, this tax allows a special deduction for long-term possession. Special deduction rates are 10 percent and 30 percent of capital gains from transfer of real estate held longer than five years and held longer than ten years, respectively. No deduction is allowed for the transfer of real estate held for less than two years or held without registration.

Although the schemes are ostensibly aimed at curbing very short-term transfers for capital gains and at stabilizing real estate prices, in practice they may actually bring about an acceleration of real estate prices through the "lock-in effect." This phenomenon takes place when property owners have an incentive to defer their tax liability by holding on to taxable property, in part because of special deductions for long-term possession. The result under the current scheme is that the capital gains tax on real estate depresses the supply of property, resulting in increased real estate prices (Kim Myung-Sook 1989b).

Moreover, although capital gains tax rates are rather high, tax yields are rather low, reflecting both a range of exemptions and deductions and the pervasive problem of undervaluation. The impact of the former is seen in table 3-7, which compares actual tax takes with revenue estimates based on measured capital gains. Whereas the average tax rates are reportedly in the 30 percent range, effective tax rates are closer to 20 percent when exemptions and deductions are considered. It is noteworthy that the capital gains tax accounted for only 16 percent of total personal income tax in 1989 and that the number of taxpayers fell between 1983 and 1989 from around 300,000 to 169,000. The major impediment to increasing substantially the revenue yield of the capital gains tax, a development that would substantially increase tax progressivity, is the undervaluation of transfer prices for land and real estate. If this undervaluation is between two-thirds and five-sixths of value (as is argued in recent studies), there is significant scope for increasing tax takes when the authorities adjust valuations. There are plans to move toward market valuations—some pronouncements refer to full market valuations by 1994—but progress to date has been slow.

Table 3-7. Capital Gains Tax on Real Estate

Year	Number of tax- payers (1,000)	Transfer amount (billion won)	Acquisi- tion amount (billion won)	Capital gains [a] (billion won) (A)	Tax base [b] (billion won) (B)	Tax Amount (billion won) (C)	Actual tax rate (percent) (C)/(B)	Effective tax rate (percent) (C)/(A)
1986	159	3,351	1,897	1,453	936	266	28.4	18.3
1987	156	2,705	1,468	1,237	820	227	27.7	18.4
1988	151	4,349	2,351	1,998	1,435	439	30.6	22.0
1989	169	6,416	3,484	2,931	2,140	724	33.8	24.7

a. Transfer amount - acquisition amount.
b. Capital gains - exemptions and deductions.
Source: Ministry of Finance (1990a).

Property Tax

The taxation of physical wealth in Korea includes an aggregate land tax on landholdings and a property tax on the holding of real properties such as dwellings, mining lots, vessels, and aircraft. The property tax is a local tax, with low rates (base rate of 0.3 percent) compared with, for example, 1.4 to 2.1 percent in Japan and 0.5 to 3.0 percent in Taiwan, China.

Aggregate Land Tax

The taxation of landholdings was carried out through the property tax until 1988, when an additional "excessive landholding tax" was introduced as a progressive tax on the aggregate of a person's holdings of unutilized urban land. From 1990 on, however, in an effort to further curb speculation on land, a new aggregate land tax took effect, consolidating the previous property tax on land and the excessive landholding tax.[9] The aggregate land tax is a progressive tax

9. Under the aggregate land tax system, all land owned by individuals and corporations is classified into three groups. The first group includes most of the

on a person's combined landholdings nationwide, and hence much more comprehensive in terms of coverage. It is expected that the aggregate land tax will not only increase tax revenue from landholding but also shift the incidence from the current system where more than half of property tax revenue is collected from the lowest tax bracket (see table 3-8).

As in the case of the capital gains tax on land, the effective tax rates are rather low because of the low assessment prices adopted by the local tax authorities.[10] The tax authorities are planning to gradually increase land assessments up to 60 percent of the local government survey value by 1994 from their current level of about 33 percent. Plans to use the 1990 Land Price Survey of 24 million pieces of land nationwide conducted by the Ministry of Construction appear stymied because these are considerably higher (perhaps by a factor of 2) than the valuations used by local tax administrations. If this revaluation took place, it would raise tax revenues from landholdings almost tenfold, up to 1,400 billion won by 1993 at current tax rates, compared with 170 billion won collected in 1988 (Kang 1990). More important, using Kang's (1990) estimates of landholdings, it would shift the incidence of the tax from the current arrangement, where the top holders pay 4.3 percent of the tax, to a situation in which this group—holding property valued at more than 20 billion won ($300 million)—would pay 24.6 percent of the land tax.

---

properties previously taxed under the excessive landholding tax, such as residential site and "idle" land, and is taxed at progressive rates ranging from 0.2 percent to 5 percent. The major difference between the current and previous systems is that, in the aggregate scheme, the nationwide landholdings of an individual or corporation are added up; in the previous scheme, progressive rates were applied to only the locally computed tax base of an individual or corporation. The second group is mainly composed of land for commercial use. The marginal tax rates are 0.2 to 2 percent and the tax brackets are much wider. The third group includes properties to be taxed at flat rates, from 0.1 percent for farmland tilled by the owner to 5.0 percent for lands for golf courses and luxurious vacation homes, regardless of the amount of land owned by a single individual or corporation.

10. The contribution of property related tax revenue to total tax revenue in Korea was only 4.3 percent in 1988, substantially lower than the 20.0 percent in Taiwan, China, and 7.1 percent in Japan. See Economic Indicators, Statistics Bureau, Taiwan, China, 1990, and Statistics of Japan, Statistics Bureau, Japan, 1988.

Table 3-8. Estimate of Aggregate Land Tax Revenue

Tax brackets	Number of taxpayers (thousand)	Hypothetical aggregate land tax (tax revenue in 1988)		Actual revenue from taxed land (holding in 1988)	
		Per taxpayer (million won)	Total (thousand won)	Per taxpayer (million won)	Total (won)
Less than 30 million won	7,964.598 (97.6)	10	77,791 (26.6)	13	99,356 (58.7)
30-100 million won	164,101 (2.0)	114	18,704 (6.4)	124	20,311 (12.0)
0.1-1 billion won	32,173 (0.4)	932	29,982 (10.3)	658	21,158 (12.5)
1-10 billion won	2,324 (0.03)	25,311	58,823 (20.1)	7,138	16,587 (9.8)
10-20 billion won	108 (0.001)	325,074	35,108 (12.0)	42,315	4,570 (2.7)
More than 20 billion won	61 (0.0007)	1,176,148	71,745 (24.6)	119,316	7,278 (4.3)
Total	8,163,365 (100.0)		292,153 (100.0)		169,260 (100.0)

Source: Kang (1990).

Inheritance and Gift Tax

The inheritance tax is imposed progressively on the total value of the estate rather than on each of the inheritances. The gift tax is imposed progressively on the cumulative value of gifts received within a three-year period. Compared with other countries, the minimum inheritance tax rate is relatively low, whereas the maximum rate is relatively high, with a smaller number of tax brackets. In addition, the number of years of accumulations for the inheritance tax is shorter than the periods in most other countries (see table 3-9).

Table 3-9. Comparison of Inheritance and Gift Tax System

Item	Korea	United States	United Kingdom	Japan	Federal Republic of Germany
Inheritance tax rate (percent)					
Minimum	10	18	30	10	3
Maximum	55	50	60	75	35
Number of brackets for inheritance tax	5	16	8	14	25
Number of years of cumulation for inheritance and gift tax	3	Lifetime	7	3	10
Inheritance tax/ total tax (percent)	0.38	0.79	0.65	1.45	0.26
Inheritance tax/GDP (percent)	0.07	0.23	0.25	0.42	0.10

Source: Kim Myung-Sook (1989a).

Despite the relatively high inheritance tax rates, the contribution of the inheritance tax to total tax revenue is very low.[11] There are two reasons for this. First, the capture ratio of inherited financial assets is very low because of the lack of a "real name" system in financial transactions. Second, the real estate assessment prices used by tax authorities average one-third of market prices, and much less in prime urban locations. As of 1989, more than 85 percent of the total value of inherited properties consisted of real estate.[12]

11. If we estimate the value of inherited wealth by utilizing the amount of collected inheritance tax (32.7 billion won), the weighted average deduction ratio (51.6 percent) and the weighted average tax rate (20.5 percent), it would amount to 330 billion won in 1987 or only 0.3 percent of GNP in 1987, which is unrealistic. This estimate is based on Kim Myung-Sook (1989a).

12. In Japan, where there is also an absence of a "real name" system, more than 70% of value of inheritance is real estate while in the U.S. the majority of wealth is in financial assets. See: Tate (1983).

Value Added Tax

Korean taxes on goods and services include the VAT and special excise taxes. The Korean VAT is a typical European Community type, with a flat rate of 10 percent on value added, which is much lower than rates used in other countries—for example, 18.6 percent in France and 18 percent in Italy.[13] Even with a relatively low VAT rate, the share of the VAT in total tax revenue in Korea, at 20 percent, is one of the highest among countries using the VAT system (Tate 1988). Nevertheless, the ratio of VAT revenue to GDP is still low, at 3.8 percent, compared with European countries—for example, 8.8 percent in France and 5.1 percent in Italy (see table 3-10).

Table 3-10. VAT as Percentage of Total Tax Revenue and GDP

Country	VAT standard rate[a] (percent)	VAT/total tax revenue (percent) (1985)	VAT/GDP (percent) (1985)
Korea	10	24.0	3.8
Indonesia	10	13.1	2.4
Morocco	19	30.4	6.5
Brazil	17	3.7	0.6
Chile	16	38.7	8.6
Uruguay	21	28.9	5.8
Turkey	15	21.9	3.2
France	18.6	22.5	8.8
Federal Republic of Germany	14	14.1	3.9
Italy	18	15.3	5.1
United Kingdom	15	17.9	6.0
Sweden	23.46	20.1	7.2

a. As of January 1, 1988.
Source: Tate (1988).

---

13. In practice, however, for the small firms with bookkeeping difficulties, the "special taxation" system is applied. Under this system, eligible firms are taxed at 0.2 percent of total annual turnover. Currently more than 70 percent of VAT payers, or 4 percent of VAT revenues, are taxed under this system. The Korean VAT has a zero-rating system, i.e., a zero tax rate with refund of the input tax incurred for items like goods for exportation, as well as exemption system, i.e., a zero tax rate without refund for items such as social welfare services.

Some Issues in Korean Taxation

Progressivity of the Korean Tax System

Although more equal distribution of income and wealth has been an objective of all tax reform efforts in Korea, it has been relatively under-emphasized in practice because the government's traditional main concern was maximization of tax revenue. The most frequently adopted measures to improve tax equity in the tax reforms have been increases of tax exemptions for low-income groups. Nevertheless, the reliance of the Korean tax system on indirect taxes, the separate taxation of most interest and dividend income at a low flat rate, the lack of a capital gains tax on financial assets, and the application of very low property assessment prices undermine the redistributive role of the Korean tax system.[14]

Consequently, it would seem that the Korean tax system as presently structured is not a major instrument of income redistribution and retains regressive elements. The perception that the poorest income groups suffer most from a higher tax burden because of the government's heavy reliance on the VAT is supported by a recent study of the 1986 tax burden (Shim and Park 1988). As shown in table 3-11 and figure 3-1, the overall tax burden is U-shaped: a substantially high tax burden (37 percent) for the first decile (the poorest); an almost flat, low (23-30 percent) burden for the second to ninth deciles; and a high (40 percent) burden on the tenth decile.[15] Government believes that the most recent tax incidence structure would be reflected in a flatter "U-shaped" curve because of recent increases in direct taxes as a share in total tax revenue, increases in the

---

14. It should be pointed out that the share of indirect taxes in total tax revenue is only one of many factors determining the progressivity of income distribution. For example, evidence in U.S. during the last 10 years shows that income distribution became less equitable despite the fact that the share of indirect taxes declined. (Source: Congressional Budget Office).

15. It is striking that the tax burden on the poorest income group is similar to that on the richest, although it is undoubtedly true that this group benefits from transfers that reduce its net tax rate. This cannot be quantified because expenditure incidence data are lacking for Korea. Other sources indicate that the Korean personal income tax system is considered less progressive than those of Thailand and Indonesia and similar to the progressivity of the systems of Malaysia and the Philippines (Virmani, 1988).

Table 3-11. Tax Burden Ratios by Income Decile, 1986

Tax burden ratio[a]	Income decile									
---	1	2	3	4	5	6	7	8	9	10
Total tax	36.89	24.67	23.00	22.49	22.84	23.44	24.35	26.51	30.14	40.13
Personal income taxes	2.20	2.04	2.26	2.62	3.29	3.83	4.39	5.91	7.75	13.20
Property taxes[b]	1.72	1.59	1.76	2.04	2.57	2.99	3.42	4.61	6.05	10.30
Corporation taxes	3.29	2.47	2.20	2.39	2.14	2.38	2.47	2.38	2.91	3.14
Indirect taxes	22.25	13.92	12.58	11.58	11.13	10.68	10.55	10.20	10.07	10.11
Customs Duties	7.43	4.65	4.20	3.86	3.71	3.56	3.52	3.41	3.36	3.38

a. Tax burden/income (percent).
b. Property tax burden structure estimated by EPB is based on the decile structure of personal income taxes.
Source: Shim and Park (1988).

Figure 3-1. Tax Burden Ratios by Income Decile
(1986)

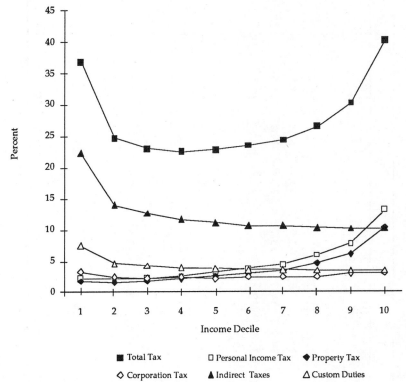

Total Tax ■ Personal Income Tax □ Property Tax ◆
Corporation Tax ◇ Indirect Taxes ▲ Custom Duties △

income tax rate on interest and dividends, and the increase in assessment values on land, but recent incidence studies are not available.

A study of the period from 1970 to 1980 found a U-shaped pattern of tax incidence, with effective tax rates for the poor and the rich higher than for the middle-income groups.[16] According to this study, the richest group shouldered a substantially heavier burden until 1976, but this pattern was reversed thereafter as the poorest income deciles bore a significantly higher tax burden (see table 3-12). This coincides with implementation of the VAT in 1977. A further study shows that

---

16. Han (1982). In contrast, Heller (1982) found a more or less proportional tax burden for 1976, before full implementation of VAT.

Table 3-12. Trend of the Tax Burden in Korea

Tax burden ratio	Income decile									
	1	2	3	4	5	6	7	8	9	10
Han Seung-Soo										
Overall tax										
1970	13.1	12.1	12.2	11.7	11.6	14.9	15.6	15.2	17.1	25.7
1976	15.7	13.4	12.9	13.0	13.0	13.4	13.4	14.5	16.4	22.8
1978	20.4	16.3	14.7	14.3	13.7	13.6	13.2	13.3	13.7	20.2
1980	28.0	19.9	17.6	16.7	15.7	15.3	14.9	14.7	14.8	20.6
Indirect taxes										
1976	15.7	13.1	12.4	11.9	11.5	11.2	10.8	10.4	9.7	9.1
1980	28.0	19.4	16.6	15.1	13.9	13.0	12.1	11.2	10.1	9.0
Direct taxes										
1970	2.3	2.4	2.7	2.4	2.5	5.9	6.7	6.4	8.4	16.8
1980	0.0	0.5	1.0	1.6	1.8	2.3	2.8	3.5	4.7	11.6
Kim Myung-Sook										
Property tax										
1985	0.54	0.42	0.39	0.35	0.38	0.42	0.42	0.45	0.54	0.64

Source: Han (1982) and Kim (1987).

the property tax burden in 1985 exhibited a flat, U-shaped pattern of tax incidence, implying that both the rich and the poor bore higher burdens than the middle-income groups, but that effective taxation was generally quite low (Kim Myung-Sook 1987). *The most important finding of these studies, particularly that of Han (1982), is that the top decile's tax burden is relatively low and is falling over time.*

Tax Evasion. The issue of tax evasion is particularly important in light of evidence that the tax system fails to capture a significant amount of various types of income, as reported in the national income accounts. As indicated in table 3-13, there are large variations among types of income in the "capture ratio," defined as income reported on tax returns as a percentage of factor income in the national income accounts. In 1983 only 40 percent of interest income and 51 percent of dividend income reported in the national income accounts were subject to taxation. *It is noteworthy that no such data is available for recent years.* Taxes were reportedly levied on only 12 percent of rental income, whereas, for example, 75 percent of employees' compensation was captured (Choi 1990).[17] [18] One reason for the low capture ratio of interest and dividend income is the lack of a "real name" system for financial transactions.[19]

---

17. In the U.S., the capture ratios of labor income, interest income, and dividend income are reportedly 97 to 98 percent, 84 to 90 percent and, 80 to 92 percent, respectively. See Choi (1987).

18. Although a high priority, it has not been possible to replicate these calculations for more recent years according to the capture ratio methodology because of a lack of data. Nor is it possible because of the Office of National Tax Administration (ONTA) data aggregation problem to assess the proportions of reported interest and dividend income that were taxed.

19. According to a recent study, the ratio of tax evasion in relation to actual tax revenue was estimated 21.4 percent in 1984. In the U.S., this ratio was estimated at 8 to 11 percent (Choi 1987).

Table 3-13. Capture Ratio by Source of Income
(percent)

Income source	1977 Tax returns/ factor income in national accounts	1983 Tax returns/ factor income in national accounts	1989 Tax returns/ factor income in national accounts
Compensation to employee	69.2	75.0	—
Property	31.6	32.1	—
Rent	16.6	11.8	—
Interest	33.4	40.2	—
Dividends	35.9-54.0	51.0	—

— Not available.
Source: Choi (1990).

Assessment. Although greater equity has been an acknowledged objective of all Korean efforts at tax reform, the major instrument of progressivity is the global income tax, a tax with redistributive clout that is limited by exemptions and by the other features of the tax system, particularly the treatment of nonwage income and the heavy reliance on indirect taxes. The net result is a tax system that can at best be described as neutral with respect to the distribution of income. In all probability, if data on earnings and addition to wealth of the upper decile were calculated and compared to tax incidence, the result would most likely be less than neutrality. Indeed, international comparisons based on table 3-5 reveal an above-average reliance in Korea on regressive taxes compared with other middle- or high-income countries. Recent government efforts—such as increases of the assessment value of land and increases in the income tax rate on interest and dividends—are expected to contribute to the progressivity of the Korean tax system.

Land and Capital Gains

Speculation on land is a serious economic and social concern in Korea. Land speculation is understandable because Korean land values, even using undervalued official prices, have increased much faster than other economic indicators such as consumer price inflation (see table 3-14). There have nevertheless been many complaints about the very concentrated ownership of land in Korea and the "unearned" capital gains from landownership. Reportedy, the top 5 percent own 65 percent of all privately owned land, whereas the bottom 40 percent own only 1 percent of the land (see table 3-15).[20] Capital gains from land, using undervalued prices, were estimated at 55 percent of GNP in 1988 (table 3-16) and were reported to be as much as GNP in 1989.[21] Moreover, 60 percent of the capital gains accruing to individuals went to the top 5 percent (see table 3-17). At the same time, low- and middle-income groups suffer from skyrocketing housing expenses as reflected in unofficial measures of housing cost (see chapter 1). These trends accelerated in 1989 and early 1990.

Table 3-14. Comparison of Land Price and Other Economic Indicators Index

Item	1975	1980	1985	1988
Land price	100.0	328.1	533.5	837.0
Housing price	100.0	355.3	397.0	447.3
Consumer price index	100.0	220.8	312.0	353.6
Bank time deposit	100.0	223.5	366.1	487.0

Source: Son (1990).

---

20. The Gini coefficient for landownership by area was estimated at 0.849, compared with the Gini coefficient for income, 0.3355, as of 1988. See Public Concept of Landownership Commission (1989).

21. Indeed, the estimates for 1988 range between 55 percent of GNP as reported by the Commission on the Public Concept of Landownership and 1.7 times GNP using market price data. (Lee 1990.)

Table 3-15. Distribution of Privately Owned Land
(percent)

Ownership	Housing sites	Factory sites	Dry fields	Paddy fields	Forestry land	Total
Top 5 percent	59.7	35.1	29.5	31.9	84.1	65.2
Top 20 percent	72.5	53.1	69.8	72.7	97.7	87.6
Bottom 40 percent	11.5	n.a.	1.6	0.4	0.1	1.0

n.a. Not available.
Note: Figures of June 1988.
Source: Public Concept of Landownership Commission (1989).

Table 3-16. Capital Gains from Land

Item	1985	1986	1987	1988
Capital gains from land (trillion won)	24.4	27.1	58.7	125.9
As percentage of GNP	31.3	29.9	55.7	101.8
As percentage of disposable income	34.4	32.7	60.9	112.0
As percentage of compensation of employees	76.4	74.7	136.8	251.1
As percentage of manufacturing value added	99.4	91.6	168.8	317.4
As percentage of central government expenditure	179.6	177.0	335.6	562.0
As percentage of fixed capital formation	106.8	105.2	190.9	348.9

Note: The figures are calculated based on the middle estimate of land value.
Source: Table 2-10.

Table 3-17. Distribution of Capital Gains from Land
(trillion won)

Category	1985	1986	1987	1988
Total capital gains from land	24.4	27.1	58.7	125.9
Gain accrued to corporates	2.4	2.9	5.9	10.7
Gain accrued to individuals	22.0	24.2	52.8	115.2
Top 5 percent	14.3	15.8	34.5	75.1
Top 10 percent	16.9	18.6	40.6	88.6
Top 25 percent	20.0	22.0	48.0	104.6

Source: Son (1990), World Bank estimates.

Public Concept of Landownership. In response to this situation, in January 1990, the Korean government introduced measures to curb ever increasing real estate speculation, to promote "economic justice" by taxing "unearned" income from real estate holdings, and to achieve efficient use of scarce land. These measures included a progressive aggregate land tax consolidating the property tax on land and the excessive landholding tax; a tax on unrealized capital gains from excessive landholding (the excessive profits tax on land holdings); a ceiling on ownership of residential land; a tax on profits from regional development projects; and regulations forcing conglomerates to sell off excessive holdings of land. These measures are called "public concept of landownership" measures.

Excess Profits Tax on Landholdings. This tax is controversial because it is levied on accrued gains rather than the realized gains. Under this system accrued net capital gains in excess of "normal" gains (the national average rate of land price increase) are taxed at 50 percent. This tax is levied wherever the land value during a one-year period exceeds 150 percent of the "normal" rate or the rate during a three-year period exceeds 100 percent of the "normal" rate. The tax applies to vacant lots, sites for vacation homes, factory sites or land attached to employee training and education facilities held by business corporations exceeding the legal limit, corporation-owned land not in proper business use, arable land owned by absentee landlords, and golf courses.

Ceiling on Ownership of Residential Land. This law sets a maximum on ownership of residential land for each household and levies a tax on the amount of land held in excess of the legal limit. Business corporations are not allowed to own residential land unless they are in the rental housing business. Households holding more land than the law permits are given two years to divest it, after which a tax is levied. The law is designed to encourage the owners of large amounts of residential land to sell, thereby expanding the ownership of land and lowering the price of land. Only 7,300 households are subject to this limit in the six largest cities, however, and there is no guarantee that the divested land will be used for residential purposes.

Tax on Profits from Regional Development Projects. This tax is levied on the increase in land value associated with such projects as residential land development, land readjustment, zoning changes, and industrial site development. The tax rate is 50 percent. A major evaluation issue exists, however, because the law stipulates that the taxable appreciation is based on the assessed value as determined by two appraisers, thus leaving room for ambiguity.

Conglomerate Holdings. It has been reported that conglomerates are heavily engaged in land speculation. Corporations own 4.1 percent of all land in Korea in area, but their share is believed to be much higher in value. Furthermore, within corporations, distribution is very concentrated; corporations owning more than 16.5 square kilometers hold 67.4 percent of total land owned by corporations (Public Concept of and Ownership Commission 1989). Capital gains accrued to corporations, although believed to be undervalued, were estimated at 4.7 percent of GNP in 1988 (Son 1990). In May 1990, Korea's forty-nine largest business groups were ordered to sell their idle and nonbusiness land and buildings within six months. They were also banned from purchasing real estate for nonbusiness purposes until June 1991. Securities and insurance firms were ordered to dispose of their excess landholdings within three months. In response, the ten top conglomerates announced that they would sell roughly 15 percent of their total real estate holdings.

Assessment. The high concentration of landholdings and the rapid increases in land prices have made landownership one of the most sensitive issues in the public fiscal debate. Reforms have been introduced, but most efforts have been aimed primarily at dampening land speculation (and the resulting surge in housing prices) rather than assuring equitable tax treatment of the returns to landholding, most of which take the form of capital gains. Official and unofficial estimates of capital gains from land are not inconsistent with an accrued value *equal to GNP*. Tax returns for transactions that are reported at admittedly undervalued assessments indicate a tax yield of 439 billion won, or 0.5 percent of GNP in 1988.[22] Ignoring for the moment the tricky issue of how to deal with unrealized capital gains, it is fairly clear that a major source of revenue is being left untapped by current practices, and that this has significant a distributional impact.

Financial Assets and Capital Gains

It is widely believed that the distribution of financial asset holdings is much more concentrated than the distribution of income. The top 10 percent reportedly owns 41 percent of total financial assets, while the bottom 40 percent owns only 8 percent as of 1988.[23] It is estimated that capital gains from stocks alone amounted to 15 percent of GNP in 1988 (KDI 1990). The Korean tax system, however, does not have the capacity to deal effectively with the issue of financial

---

22. It is difficult to estimate the potential tax yield on capital gains because assessments are biased and evasion is obviously a major factor. Nevertheless, because land prices rose 27.5 percent in 1988 and using independent estimates that 7.6 percent of plots changed hands in 1988 yields a realized gross capital gain of 9.3 trillion won using total landholdings of 444 trillion won (see land estimate in table 2-6). Assuming an average capital gains tax rate of 50 percent, one could expect capital gains tax revenue of 4.7 trillion won, which is ten times higher than actual tax revenue collected in that year (see table 3-7).

23. This estimate is based on Bank of Korea (1988). According to BOK's survey, the Gini coefficient of financial assets in 1988 is 0.561, much higher than the Gini coefficient of income, 0.3355. Moreover, KDI's survey shows even more concentrated distribution; the top 10 percent owned 78 percent while the bottom 40 percent owned almost nothing. In turn, National Citizen Bank's survey shows similar result to BOK's.

assets: there is no capital gains tax on financial asset transactions and most interest and dividend income is taxed separately at a low flat rate. These favorable tax incentives were originally adopted to mobilize necessary domestic funds through official financial markets and to discourage the curb market that flourished in the 1960s and 1970s. Recently, however, the situation has turned around: the stock market was booming, the curb market almost disappeared, and the trade balance was in surplus.

In response to these new favorable developments and to complaints from middle- and low-income groups on unequal distribution of wealth, the government announced reform measures effective January 1, 1991 to include: (i) a "real name" system whereby asset holders are forced to use their own names in financial transactions;[24] (ii) gradual introduction of global progressive taxation of interest and dividend income starting with high interest and dividend income earners;[25] and (iii) step-by-step introduction of a capital gains tax on stock transactions starting with major stockholders.[26] Nonetheless, faced with the economy's poor performance in 1989 and early 1990, skyrocketing real estate prices, fear of capital flight, and strong resistance from conglomerates, the government canceled the scheduled implementation of reform measures in early 1990.

Opponents of these reforms argue that it is still premature to implement the reforms because the domestic financial market is not sufficiently mature, with a ratio of financial assets to GNP of 3.7 compared with 6.8 in Japan.[27] They argue that the government should first concentrate on curbing speculation in real estate by implementing

---

24. Similarly, in 1982, as an aftermath of a huge financial scandal, a law banning fictitious name financial transactions was passed by the National Assembly but with a proviso that actual implementation would be suspended until the economy gained sufficient strength and an efficient administration was established. The government never launched the system.

25. According to Kang's (1990) estimate, global taxation of interest and dividend income at 25 percent (rather than the separate 10 percent tax) would have raised 630 billion won more in 1988, or 2.7 percent of actual total tax collection.

26. Kang (1990) estimated the amount of tax revenue that would be generated by a capital gains tax on stock revenue transactions. Assuming a 20 percent tax rate, 2,050 billion won of tax revenue would be obtained, or 8.7 percent of actual total tax collection in 1988.

27. Japan intended to implement a real name system (called the "Green Card" System) in 1984, but never followed through with it.

the aggregate land tax and increasing assessment prices. Proponents of the reforms argue that (i) by postponing the reforms twice in less than ten years the government is showing a lack of credibility in implementing economic policies; (ii) the adverse effects of the reforms could be avoided through gradual, step-by-step implementation;[28] and (iii) the cost of implementing the reforms later will be much higher, considering the imminent opening up of the capital market and the expected further financial deepening.

Assessment. While it is difficult to measure the financial asset holdings of the populace, the personal wealth balance sheet approach provides an order of magnitude (table 2-11). If gross financial assets are 138 trillion won and the average yield on those assets in 1988 was 15 percent, which is not unrealistic, gross returns (income) would have been about 20 trillion won. Even if one used a net financial asset figure (deducting financial debts), the total yield gained by holders of financial wealth would have been 12 trillion won. Because at least 43 percent (perhaps as high as 61 percent) of these assets are reportedly held by the top income decile and perhaps two-thirds are held by the top two deciles, a reasonable 50 percent tax rate would yield an expected income tax take of 6 million won, which exceeds total direct income generated from all sources. This points to a healthy dose of evasion, mostly by the upper-income groups who hold these assets and demonstrates, at least illustratively, the large untapped potential of effectively taxing financial assets.

1990 Tax Reform

The Korean government introduced new tax reforms effective January 1, 1991 to gain a more balanced tax burden across different kinds of income and income groups, more realistic tax rates and deductions to encourage honest tax reporting, rationalization of corporate taxes to enhance competitiveness, and adjustment of the tax

---

28. Taiwan, China, reintroduced a capital gains tax on stock transactions (initially introduced in 1974 and then suspended in 1976). When the government announced the introduction of this tax in September 1988, the stock price index plummeted from 8,800 to 5,600 in one month. With some relaxation of the initial proposal, however, the stock price index rose to 10,000 by June 1989. See Korea Development Institute (1990).

system to compensate for the expired defense tax and temporary education tax.

According to the reform, the highest global income tax rate was cut from 60 percent to 50 percent. At the same time, the number of income brackets was decreased from eight to five. Deductions for wages and salaries were increased from 2.3 million won to 4.9 million won. The government also increased the deduction for medical expenses and introduced a deduction for housing rents for the approximately 1.7 million workers earning less than 1 million won (US$1,400) a month and lacking their own dwellings. The government increased the tax rate on interest and dividend income under real names from 16-17 percent to 20 percent. For interest and dividend income under "fictitious" names, a 60 percent tax rate is applied. Current corporate tax rates vary from 24 percent to 41.25 percent depending on the type of corporation. The government introduced simpler and lower tax rates: 20 percent for corporations with a tax base of less than 100 million won and 34 percent for tax base exceeding 100 million won.

The government strengthened the inheritance and gift taxes. It implemented an inheritance tax period of ten years rather than the previous five years. It raised the minimum rate, lowered the maximum rate, and reduced the number of brackets: a 10-55 percent inheritance tax with five brackets rather than the previous 6-66 percent with eight brackets. In addition, the government strengthened the capital gains tax on real estate. It limited the total combined amount of deductions on capital gains to 30 million won. There was no limit under the previous system. Last, the government intended to gain the lost revenue of defense tax, which expired at the end of 1990, from other major taxes and changed the status of the education tax from a temporary to a permanent tax.

Assessment. The expected impact of these reforms should not be very large. For example, a substantial increase in revenue is not expected from the slight increase of the tax rate on interest and dividend income, but the revenue loss from decreases in the income and corporate tax rates is also expected to be small. There could be a slight improvement in distribution because of the lower tax rate on labor income, more deductions for low-income groups, a higher tax rate on interest and dividend income, and strengthened inheritance and gift taxes. No major improvement is expected in reporting. In light of the larger issues raised with respect to effective taxation of all sources of income and a broader sharing of the tax burden, especially by the highest income group, these reforms are unlikely to significantly alter the current situation.

A Comparison of Previous and New Tax Schedules		
	Previous [a] *(percent)*	*New (percent)*
Income tax	5.5-60 8 brackets	5-50 5 brackets
Inheritance tax	6-66 8 brackets	10-55 5 brackets
Gift tax	6-72 8 brackets	15-60 5 brackets
Corporation tax		
Listed corporation	24-37.5	
Nonlisted large corporation	24-41.25	20-34
Nonprofit corporation	24-33.75	
Cooperatives	10.5-14.5	10
Other public corporation	15-23.25	17-25
Interest & dividend tax		
Real name	16-17	20
Fictitious name	49-53	60

a. Including defense tax.

Policy Options

The evidence reviewed in the previous chapters suggests that the enormous economic gains that Korea has achieved over the past twenty-five years have not been appropriated by a single group of individuals. All segments of society have experienced a dramatic improvement in their standard of living. The increase in income inequality normally associated with this stage of development has not apparently taken place in Korea, or at least has not taken place to the extent that would have been predicted. At the same time it is clear that a small proportion of the population has made spectacular advances in a relatively short period of time, accumulating fortunes that are large by any standards through their holdings of land and corporate stock.

When assessing the Korean performance in the distributional area against that of other countries, two special features should be taken into account. First, a high proportion of the benefits of economic growth have been captured in asset appreciation, in part a result of deliberate government policy to restrain the cost of finance, and hence interest rates. There is a strong suspicion that measured income inequality is distorted by this high level of asset appreciation in relation to income flows. If a realistic estimate of accrued capital gains from real estate and corporate assets were included in the definition of income, or if a reasonable rate of return was imputed to wealth, the trend in the distribution of income in recent years would quite probably show the increase in inequality that many people believe has occurred. The suggestion that inequality may be incompletely measured cautions against a complacent attitude toward the Korean performance.

The second special feature is the homogenous and generally class-less nature of Korean society, which perhaps makes the population more conscious of differences in living standards and more concerned about inequality. This concern is typically expressed in terms of the overall spread of living standards and the similarity of treatment of people in similar initial circumstances. There is clearly widespread resentment at vertical inequity directed not so much at the hardship of the poor, but at the privileges of the rich. Horizontal equity is also a cause for complaint, for instance, in the tax treatment of business income compared with wages and salaries. Rapid economic growth and improvements in average living standards go a long way toward keeping such feelings in check. But if growth declines for any appreciable length of time, popular resentment may well be expressed more forcefully.

The challenge facing Korea, therefore, is to discover a means of removing horizontal anomalies and improving the relative position of middle- and low-income groups without detriment to the prospects for future growth. In this respect the current system of taxation, and public policy in general, merits reexamination. The overall impact of taxation is barely neutral for measured income, and it is almost certainly regressive with respect to a more comprehensive definition of income. It has therefore reinforced, rather than ameliorated, the inequalities generated by market forces.

There is little cause for criticism in the overall coverage of tax programs. Virtually everything that could provide a source of revenue is exploited for that purpose, the only notable exception being capital gains on financial transactions. Nevertheless, the tax system has been designed primarily to raise revenue and to support the government's expansionist economic policies. Little consideration has been given to its redistributive role or to the way that the different programs interact. Studies of tax incidence are at a rudimentary level. More important, the data necessary for a reliable assessment of the redistributive impact of the government sector do not appear to be collected. For instance, ONTA is unable to provide a breakdown of income tax payments by income level, or a breakdown of the global income tax base by income source. An immediate priority, therefore, is to review the data necessary for a reliable assessment of tax incidence and to ensure that the data are made available to those who could analyze them profitably. The authorities should aim for a consolidated, decile-by-decile accounting for all taxes paid as the basic analytic underpinning needed to pursue equity issues in the Korean context, such as that provided for the U.S. tax system by income decile (see Pechman 1985 and Pechman and Okner 1974 for the approach). This should be supplemented by much more detailed tax incidence data collection for nonwage income sources.

Income Taxation

Many of the changes that have taken place over the past few years or are proposed to take place in the immediate future are steps in the right direction. The trend toward taking a larger share of tax revenue from income taxation, and from direct taxation in general, and a smaller share from indirect taxation will probably continue, and rightly so. The simplification of the global income tax schedule is also welcome, although much more could be done by removing many of the special allowances and adjusting the rates accordingly. Complicated systems of allowances encourage tax avoidance and inefficiency, which probably more than offset the benefits to other objectives of government policy. The proposed reduction in the top marginal income tax rate from 60 percent to 50 percent, together with the removal of the defense tax surcharge, is also sensible. Although it may nominally appear to make the tax system less progressive, evidence from other countries suggests that marginal tax rates in excess of 50 percent may be counterproductive, encouraging avoidance and downright dishonesty.

One reform that is long overdue is legislation to bring the treatment of business income into line with income from other sources, either by requiring businesses to report actual surpluses or, failing that, to ensure that allowances for business costs accurately reflect actual expenditures. The current flat rate tax on interest and dividends also appears to introduce horizontal inequity into the treatment of income from different sources, although the data available do not permit an assessment of the quantitative significance of underreporting of interest and dividend income for global income tax purposes. Legislation to insist on the use of real names in financial transactions would help to minimize tax avoidance on these items, and the indefinite postponement of this legislation leaves the government open to criticism that it is not sufficiently concerned with tax evasion. If the "real name" legislation is not introduced, there is a case for further raising the withholding tax on interest and dividends, in part to balance the raised exemption level for wages and salaries. The impact on the savings of small investors could be offset by allowing everyone to nominate a single savings account on which the first one million won of interest would be tax exempt.

Consumption Taxes

The value added tax is operating successfully, and there is no compelling reason to change the current arrangements. The decline in the proportion of tax revenue raised by VAT observed in recent years seems set to continue, so its regressive impact will decline in significance. Regarding customs duties and the special excise tax, the very high rates on luxury imported goods may well attract undue attention from Korea's trading partners and will probably need to be revised downward in the medium term. (At a minimum, there should be no distinction between luxury taxes on imports and domestic luxuries.) This will tend to increase the regressivity of consumption taxes, making it even more imperative to strengthen the progressive impact of other taxes.

Taxation of Wealth

The key to distributional fairness within a thriving and prosperous Korean economy lies with the attitude toward wealth ownership—not only taxes on land and other forms of property, both real and financial, but also positive measures designed to encourage the spread of wealth among low- and middle-income groups, so that all sections of society participate in, and benefit from, rises in asset prices. This is hardly the case now. In recent years, low-income groups have found themselves in a situation where their own modest assets invested in savings accounts receive a modest real rate of return, while the value of real estate holdings, and the rents they generate, rise precipitously.

Recent legislation on property taxation is certainly helpful. It makes sense, for example, to aggregate all domestic landholdings together, as is done in the Aggregate Land Tax, rather than to levy taxes on a regional basis. Taxing accrued rather than realized capital gains on land and taking a share in development rights, through the tax on profits from regional development projects, are also to be commended. There is a suspicion that these measures are directed at the symptoms, however, rather than the causes of land price inflation. As long as land for residential and industrial use is strictly rationed, and finance is cheap, investment in land will look attractive compared with other assets, and resentment will continue to grow among those who are unable to benefit from land price rises.

There is little doubt that evasion of the capital gains tax on real estate has taken place on a large scale in recent years. No other plausible explanation comes to mind for the very low yield of capital gains tax in relation to the estimates of accrued gains. The project being undertaken by the Ministry of Construction to value every plot of land in the country, and to revise these prices every year on the basis of a sample survey, is ambitious and will help to determine true gains. The planned rise in assessed values will also remove an element of discretion, and hence a potential source of tax avoidance. There is much to be said in favor of a speedy move all the way to actual market prices, while at the same time revising the tax rates slightly downward to reduce the burden on lower-income groups.[29] Deliberate tax evasion could be overcome by calculating capital gains on the difference between the current price and the price at which the property was last registered. It is also suggested that the government conduct a survey of a number of land plots, tracing ownership back over the past ten years, to determine the degree of tax evasion that has taken place and how it has been accomplished. This might be preceded by a well-publicized period of amnesty for those wishing to report a previously unrecorded tax liability.

One problem with property taxation in recent years is that too much emphasis is placed on taxing transfers of property and increases in property value rather than taxing the total value of holdings. Comparing, for example, the tax yield from registration and acquisition taxes on real property in 1988 to yields from the property tax itself shows it to be five times larger. This means that an individual who chooses to keep his property is taxed much more lightly than one who buys and sells. Although this bias in taxation is intended to discourage speculation, it also penalizes those with more laudable motives. Furthermore, it has been argued that it may actually contribute to the acceleration of real estate prices by encouraging individuals to hoard property to reduce their tax liability, and hence depress the supply of real estate for sale.

Any attempt to strengthen capital gains legislation carries with it the danger that current wealth inequalities will be locked in. This possibility can be counteracted by raising the exemptions on the capital gains tax, the registration tax, and the acquisition tax and

29. It should be noted that current reforms aim at reaching assessments equal to 100 percent of market value for capital gains but only 60 percent of local government survey value (30 percent of market value) for local property tax calculations. This inconsistency should be eliminated and adjustments made in the relevant tax rates.

offsetting the loss of revenue by a rise in taxes directed at the total wealth holdings of the very rich. An ultimate goal could be the replacement of the aggregate land tax with a full-fledged net wealth tax, levied on the aggregate of both real estate and financial wealth.[30] The present treatment of corporate stock seems especially generous in view of the personal fortunes obviously amassed in Korea in recent years. It is not intended that the tax rates should be high, or that the vast majority of the population would be liable. A marginal tax rate of 1 percent on assets over 500 million won, for example, with higher rates at, say 1 billion won and 10 billion won, would be sufficient.

As already indicated, a tax on capital gains from financial assets is the most obvious omission from the otherwise comprehensive system of taxes in Korea. One strong argument in favor of such a tax is the distortion it introduces into the decisions of companies and individual investors. For example, it gives corporations an incentive to retain earnings and seek appreciation of share prices rather than pay dividends. Because this is consistent with other government objectives, the redistributional implications may not weigh heavily. Corporate stockholdings are, of course, taxed indirectly through the corporation tax. If financial wealth is covered by a wealth tax in the way suggested, the argument for a separate tax on capital gains would be fairly weak. It remains, however, a further potential source of revenue to offset losses from other sources.

The inheritance and gift taxes do not make a major contribution to either tax revenue or redistribution. Nevertheless, their importance is likely to grow as the major wealth holdings accumulated during the past twenty-five years are passed on to the next generation. The proposed extension of the period prior to death during which gifts are included in the value of estates is sensible, and there is no compelling need to make other changes at this time apart from raising land valuations toward market values and monitoring aherence to inheritance tax regulations.

---

30. There are seventeen countries that implement net wealth taxes, including India and Pakistan in addition to some European countries such as Germany, Netherlands, Austria, Switzerland, and the Nordics. (Due and Friedlaender 1981).

Other Special Measures

There are a number of other measures that could have a significant beneficial effect on income and wealth distribution in the longer run and are consistent with other government objectives, as well as being potentially useful to the maintenance of social harmony. Although a rudimentary employee share ownership scheme was already introduced in Korea, it could be strengthened in the context of improved labor-management relations. As an illustrative example, the government could encourage firms to distribute 1 percent of their shares each year among their employees and allow the value of these shares to be deducted from the base for corporation tax liability. Employees could be required to hold their shares for a minimum of five years, and allowed to receive their dividends free of tax. From the government's point of view, the loss of tax revenue may be more than amply rewarded by greater industrial harmony and the participation of a much broader section of the population in increases in corporate wealth.

Other progressive measures would be those designed to aid the spread of homeownership to enable more households to benefit from real estate appreciation. Experience in other countries suggests that the rise in owner occupancy has had a major impact on long-term wealth equality. This might be encouraged by exempting owner-occupied housing (one unit per family) from the capital gains, registration, and acquisition taxes, thus reducing the impact of these taxes as recommended earlier. Further measures would be necessary to give more households access to mortgage finance, which is typically provided in Korea by relatives and friends. Alternative sources of finance—either banks or mortgage finance institutions—would need to be developed and perhaps encouraged by tax concessions or direct government assistance, possibly at the local level, to lower-income groups. Such measures will tend to fuel demand for real estate, and may not therefore be favored now. In the longer run, however, they provide attractive options.

The final option to be considered is the accumulation of nontangible wealth in the form of pension rights. It has already been seen that social security contributions and pension wealth are at a very low level in Korea, and demands will undoubtedly increase in this area. Pension entitlements are a close substitute for many forms of income-generating assets, and they tend to be much more equally distributed than any other kind of asset. So any move toward a national pension scheme offering a reasonable level of benefits is likely to have a major impact on the distribution of wealth, broadly defined.

There is no dearth of tax reform proposals in Korea, and this report certainly adds to that menu of options. The basic premise for reforms is that the very rapid growth of income, and more particularly wealth, has led to a loss of momentum in the pursuit of equitable growth. Some of this is inevitable, and will have to be offset with transfers for the lowest income groups. Nevertheless, for the highest income group, care must be taken to limit the windfall nature of gains from wealth holdings if the essential fabric of Korean society, which has provided for such monumental strides in economic performance, is to remain intact.

Policy Lessons

Although many policy lessons within taxation may be unique to Korea, there are other aspects that may be symptomatic of rapidly growing economies. In the process of rapid industrialization, the financial sector is often the lagging sector. Certainly this has been the experience of Korea, and to a lesser extent in Thailand and Malaysia. As financial deepening takes place, tax policy toward financial assets needs to be reexamined. In Korea, the run-up in stock prices, spiraling real estate prices, and the importance more generally of financial assets has not yet been matched by effective taxation of capital gains. To the contrary, twice in the last decade the government has shied away from introducing a "real name system" for financial transactions and no capital gains tax on financial assets has been instituted.

This has raised issues of both horizontal and vertical equity. There is a perception in Korea and in other rapidly growing economies that wage earners are taxed more effectively than interest earners. Indeed, even in the United States, gains at the upper end of the income distribution in the last decade are associated with changes in capital gains rather than earned incomes.[31] Although Korea operates under a global income concept, it has not provided the kind of progressivity that many desire because of certain features, including: (a) no capital gains tax on financial assets; (b) a separate, low flat tax rate on interest and dividend income; (c) some differentiation in treatment of self-employed professional incomes versus wage income; (d) weak treatment of capital gains from real estate transactions; and (e) loopholes that limit the effectiveness of inheritance taxes.

The Korean authorities have realized that the current system is no longer adequate in light of the very substantial income gains of the past decade. Remedial measures are now under way in response to public complaints about fairness. The previous section on wealth gains has documented how rapidly growing economies can see decades of relative equality in incomes being threatened by passive taxation methods, methods that were primarily designed to generate revenue rather than affect relative incomes. There is a new realization in Korea that each aspect of tax reform must be examined for its distributional consequences. Although the imposition of a presumptive assessment on high-income households was shelved as part of the 1990 tax reform, the issue of personal wealth accumulation is central to the public policy debate and will require attention in a number of rapidly industrializing economies.

Tax policy is seen as part of the national fabric, and if it is not taken seriously can lead to social disharmony. Particularly in countries like Korea, where labor productivity has been extraordinarily high, imperfections in the tax system can spill over into poor labor-management relations. Countries in the region are now experimenting with flexi-wage systems, to share between owners of capital and labor the benefits of productivity gains. Without reasonable equity in the tax system, however, these will be futile efforts. Korea is now learning that lesson.

---

31. According to the Center on Budget and Policy Priorities (1990), the top 1 percent of the U.S. income distribution saw its income rise by 87.1 percent between 1980 and 1990, driven largely by a 116.6 percent rise in capital gains income.

BIBLIOGRAPHY

Adelman, Irma. 1974. "Redistribution with Growth: Some Country Experiences-
-The Case of Korea." In Hollis Chenery and others, eds., *Redistribution with
Growth*. London: Oxford University Press.

Adelman, I., and S. Robinson. 1978. *Income Distribution Policy in Developing
Countries: A Case Study of Korea*. London: Oxford University Press.

Ahluwalia, M. 1976. "Inequality, Poverty, and Development," *Journal of
Development Economics* 3: 307-42.

Atkinson, A. B., and A. J. Harrison. 1978a. *Distribution of Personal Wealth in
Britain*. Cambridge: Cambridge University Press.

Atkinson, A. B., and A. J. Harrison. 1978b. "Wealth." In W. F. Maunder, ed.,
Reviews of United Kingdom Statistical Sources, Vol. 6. Oxford: Pergamon.

Bank of Korea. 1988. *Household Deposits Survey*.

_____. 1990. *Economic Statistics Yearbook*.

Bhalla, Surjit S. 1979. "The Distribution of Income in Korea: A Critique and a
Reassessment." Mimeo. World Bank, Washington, D.C.

Center on Budget and Policy Priorities. 1990. *Drifting Apart: New Findings on
Growing Income Disparities*, Washington D.C.

Chenery, Hollis, and others. 1974. *Redistribution with Growth*. London: Oxford
University Press.

Choi Kwang. 1987. *A Study on Underground Economy in Korea*. Korea
Economic Research Institute [in Korean].

_____. 1990. "Tax Policy and Tax Reforms in Korea." Paper presented at
World Bank Conference on Tax Policy in Developing Countries, March
1990, Washington, D.C.

Choo, Hakchung. 1985. "Estimation of Size Distribution of Income and Its
Sources of Change in Korea, 1982." KDI Working Paper 8515.

Choo, H., and J. Yoon. 1984. "Size Distribution of Income in Korea, 1982: Its
Estimation and Sources of Change." [in Korean], *Korea Development Review*
6 (March): 2-18.

Citizen's National Bank. 1988. *Household Finance Survey*.

Commission on Tax Reform. 1985. Seoul. "The Final Report of the Commission on Tax Reform."

Daewoo Securities. 1989. "Investment Survey of 160 Companies in the Korean Stock Market."

_____. 1990. "The Korean Economy & the Securities Market."

Davies, J. B. 1979. "On the Size Distribution of Wealth in Canada." *Review of Income and Wealth.*

Due, J. F. and A. F. Friedlaender. 1981. *Government Finance: Economics of the Public Sector.* Richard D. Irwin.

Greenwood, D. T. 1987. "Age, Income, and Household Size: Their Relation to Wealth Distribution in the United States." In E. N. Woolf, ed., *International Comparisons of the Distribution of Household Wealth.* London: Oxford University Press.

Han Seung-Soo. 1982. *Empirical Analysis of Tax Burden in Korea and Theoretical Analysis of Optimal Tax Burden.* Korea Economic Research Institute. [In Korean]

Harrison, A. J. 1979. "The Distribution of Wealth in Ten Countries." Background Paper No. 7, Royal Commission on the Distribution of Income and Wealth. London: HMSO.

Heller, P. S. 1982. *The Incidence of Taxation in Korea.* Departmental memorandum 81/14. International Monetary Fund: Washington, D.C.

Hong Wontack. 1990. "Land Problem in Korea and Policy Directions." [In Korean]

IMF. 1990. *International Financial Statistics.* Washington, D.C.

_____. Various years. *Government Finance Statistics Yearbook.* Washington, D.C.

Japan, Statistics Bureau. 1988. *Statistics of Japan.*

Kang Bong-Gyun. 1990. "The Impact of Economic Development Strategy in Size Distribution of Income in Korea." Ph.D. diss. Hanyang University. [In Korean]

Kessler, D. and A. Masson. 1987. "Personal Wealth Distribution in France: Cross-Sectional Evidence and Extensions." In E. N. Woolf, ed., *International Comparisons of the Distribution of Household Wealth.* London: Oxford University Press.

Kim, D., and K. S. Ahn. 1987. *Korea's Income Distribution, Its Determinants, and People's Consciousness about Distribution Problems.* Seoul: Jung Ang University Press. [In Korean]

Kim Kyung-Hwan. 1991. *Housing Prices, Affordability, and Government Policy in Korea.* World Bank Discussion Paper. Washington, D.C.

Kim Myung-Sook. 1987. *Distributive Effects of Property Tax in Korea.* Korea Development Institute. [In Korean].

_____. 1989a. *Current Status and Reform of Inheritance and Gift Tax.* Korea Development Institute. [In Korean].

_____. 1989b. *Lock-in-effect of Capital Gains Tax on Real Estate and Recommendations for Reform.* Korea Development Institute. [In Korean]

Korean Commission on the Public Concept of Land Ownership. 1989, 1990. "Report on the Public Concept of Land Ownership."

Korea Development Institute. 1989. *Report of Commission for More Equal Distribution of Income and Wealth.* [In Korean]

_____. 1990. *Impact of Real Name System.* [In Korean]

Korea, Economic Planning Board. Various years. *National Wealth Survey.*

Korea, Economic Planning Board. 1988. *Social Indicators of Korea.*

Korea, Housing Bank. Various years. *Housing Finance Bimonthly Review.*

Korea, Ministry of Finance. 1990a. *Major Tax Statistics.* Seoul.

_____. 1990b. *Korean Taxation.* Seoul.

_____. 1990c. *1990 Tax Reform Proposal.* Seoul. [In Korean]

Korea, Office of National Tax Administration. 1989. *Statistical Yearbook of National Tax.* Seoul.

Kuznets, Simon. 1955. "Economic Growth and Income Inequality." *American Economic Review* 45 (March): 1-28.

Kwack Tae-Won and Lee Kye-Sik. 1990. *Tax Reform in Korea.* (Processed).

Kwon Soonwon. 1990. "Korea: Income Distribution and Government Initiatives to Reduce Disparities." Korea Development Institute.

Lee, Jin Soon. 1990. "System of Land Ownership and Use." Seoul. (Processed).

Leechor, C. 1986. *Tax Policy and Tax Reform in Semi-Industrial Countries,* Industry and Finance Series, Vol. 13. World Bank: Washington, D.C.

Leipziger, Danny M. 1988. "Industrial Restructuring in Korea." *World Development* 16 (No. 1): 121-36.

Leipziger, Danny M., and Peter A. Petri. 1988. "Korean Incentive Policies toward Industry and Agriculture." In J. G. Williamson and V. R. Panchamukhi, eds., *The Balance Between Industry in Economic Development.* New York: MacMillan.

Moon, P. Y. and B. S. Kang. 1986. "A Comparative Study of the Political Economy of Agricultural Policies: The Case of South Korea." World Bank, Washington, D.C.

Pechman, J., and B. Okner. 1974. *Who Bears the Tax Burden.* Washington, D.C.: The Brookings Institution.

Pechman, Joseph A. 1985. *Who Paid the Taxes, 1966-85?* Washington, D.C.: The Brookings Institution.

_____. 1990. "Why We Should Stick with the Income Tax." *The Brookings Review* (Spring).

Shalizi, Z. 1989. *Commodity Taxation in Selected Countries in South East and East Asia.* Asia Region Internal Discussion Paper 37, World Bank: Washington, D.C.

Shim, Sang-Dahl. 1989. *An Analysis of Benefit Distribution of Government Expenditure.* Korea Development Institute. [In Korean]

Shim, Sang-Dahl and Nam Sang-Woo. 1988. *Guidelines for Public Finance Management for Economic Stabilization and Welfare Improvement.* Korea Development Institute. [In Korean]

Shim, Sang-Dahl and Park In-Won. 1988. *Public Finance and Income Redistribution.* Working Paper, Korea Development Institute, Seoul. [In Korean]

Shorrocks, A. F. 1975. "The Age-Wealth Relationship: A Cross-Section and Cohort Analysis", *Review of Economics and Statistics,* 57(2): 155-163.

_____. 1987. "UK Wealth Distribution: Current Evidence and Future Prospects." In E. N. Woolf, ed., *International Comparisons of the Distribution of Household Wealth.* London: Oxford University Press.

Sicat, G. P., and A. Virmani. 1988. "Personal Income Taxes in Developing Countries." *The World Bank Economic Review* (January).

_____. 1989. *Personal Income Taxes in Developing Countries: International Comparisons.* DRD Discussion Paper 265. World Bank, Washington, D.C.

Son Jae-Young. 1990. *An Analysis of Land Problem and Recommendations.* Korea Development Institute. [In Korean]

Spant, R. 1987. "Wealth Distribution in Sweden: 1920-1983." In E. N. Woolf, ed., *International Comparisons of the Distribution of Household Wealth.* London: Oxford University Press.

Suh, Sang-Mok. 1985. "Economic Growth and Change in Income Distribution: The Korean Case." Korea Development Institute Working Paper 8508.

Summers, Robert, and Alan Heston. 1988. "A New Set of International Comparisons of Real Product and Price Levels: Estimates for 130 Countries, 1950-1985." *Review of Income and Wealth* 34 (March): 1-25.

Tachibanaki. 1989. "Japan's New Policy Agenda: Coping with Unequal Asset Distribution." *Journal of Japanese Studies:* 345-369.

Taiwan, China, Statistics Bureau. 1990. *Economic Indicators.*

Tanzi, V. 1987. "Quantitative Characteristics of the Tax Systems." In D. Newberry and N. Stern, eds., *Theory of Taxation for Developing Countries.* London: Oxford University Press.

Tate, A. A. 1983. "Net Wealth, Gift and Transfer Taxes." *Comparative Tax Studies.*

_____. 1988. *Value-Added Tax, International Practice and Problems.* Washington, D.C.: International Monetary Fund.

United States, Congressional Budget Office. 1990. "Distributional Effects of the Administration's Capital Gains Proposal". Washington, D.C.

Virmani, A. 1988. *Direct Taxes and Fiscal Policy Issues: An Illustration for East Asia.* Asia Region Internal Discussion Paper 36. World Bank, Washington, D.C.

Woolf, E. N., ed. 1987. *International Comparisons of the Distribution of Household Wealth.* Oxford: Oxford University Press.

World Bank. 1987. *Korea: Managing the Industrial Transition.* Washington, D.C.

_____. 1989. *Social Indicators of Development.* Washington, D.C.

_____. 1990. Malaysia: Growth, Poverty Alleviation, and Improved Income Distribution", Report 8667-MA. Washington, D.C.

_____. 1990. *Value-Added Taxation in Developing Countries.* M. Gillis, C. S. Shoup, and G. P. Sicat, eds. Washington, D.C.

_____. 1991. *Lessons of Tax Reform.* Washington, D.C.

_____. Various years. *World Development Report.* New York: Oxford University Press.

INDEX

(Page numbers in italics indicate material in tables or figures.)